# PRACTICAL SUGGESTIONS FOR TEACHING

*Edited by* Alice Miel

———————•———————

## PHONICS AND THE TEACHING OF READING

# TITLES IN THIS SERIES

Science Experiences for Elementary Schools     *Charles K. Arey*

Individual Parent-Teacher Conferences     *Katherine E. D'Evelyn*

Pupil Progress in the Elementary School     *Willard S. Elsbree*

Individualizing Reading Practices     *Alice Miel, Editor*

Building Children's Science Concepts     *Mary Sheckles*

Improving Children's Facility in Problem Solving     *Alma Bingham*

A Classroom Teacher's Guide to Physical Education     *C. Eric Pearson*

Observing and Recording the Behavior of Young Children
    *Dorothy H. Cohen and Virginia Stern*

Helping Children in Oral Communication     *Alberta Munkres*

Helping Children Accept Themselves and Others     *Helen L. Gillham*

Independent Activities for Creative Learning
    *Helen Fisher Darrow and R. Van Allen*

Phonics and the Teaching of Reading     *Dolores Durkin*

Reading Improvement in the Junior High School     *Deborah Elkins*

Learning Through Movement     *Betty Rowen*

Social Studies for Understanding     *Helen Fisher Darrow*

# PHONICS

## and the Teaching of Reading

### SECOND EDITION

#### DOLORES DURKIN

ASSOCIATE PROFESSOR OF EDUCATION
TEACHERS COLLEGE, COLUMBIA UNIVERSITY

TEACHERS COLLEGE PRESS
TEACHERS COLLEGE, COLUMBIA UNIVERSITY
NEW YORK

© 1962, 1965 BY TEACHERS COLLEGE, COLUMBIA UNIVERSITY

LIBRARY OF CONGRESS CATALOG CARD NUMBER: 65-16543

SECOND PRINTING, 1966

PRINTED IN THE UNITED STATES OF AMERICA

# Editor's Introduction

For much of this century there has been a running argument between those who seem to believe that a phonetic approach alone should be employed in teaching beginning reading and others who are extremely dubious about using such an approach too early and too exclusively. The latter do not claim that children should be taught no phonics at all in learning to read. They merely want to reverse the order of events traditionally associated with the teaching of reading in the days of the *New England Primer* and the McGuffey Readers. Instead of beginning with the alphabet and isolated sounds of letters and syllables, they advocate introducing children first to meaningful wholes—words, phrases, and sentences that communicate an intelligible message. Then gradually children are to be helped to gain control over the component parts— the syllables and letters with their varying sounds.

The author of this book wants children to learn to read and wants them to learn efficiently. This desire she shares with the advocates of various phonics systems. She too assigns an important role to phonics in reading instruction. It is to state a reasoned and well-supported position on the use of phonics in teaching reading and to give help to teachers as they introduce their children to the intricacies of printed American English that this book has been prepared. Professor Durkin knows how to teach children to read and how to teach teachers of reading. She knows the research in her field and she has made a critical assessment of the claims and counterclaims so prevalent today. She has done a real service to the field of reading instruction in writing this lucid and sensible analysis of the place of phonics.

ALICE MIEL

# Contents

EDITOR'S INTRODUCTION    V

1. INTRODUCTION    1

What Is Phonics?    1
Phonics and the English Language    2
Development of the English Language    2
Pronunciation Variations in Our Language    4
Meaning of Language Irregularities for Teachers    5

2. THE CONTROVERSIAL HISTORY OF PHONICS    8

Early History of Phonics    8
Later Developments    9
The Current Scene    10
Phonics as *the* Method of Teaching Reading    10
Phonics as One Kind of Help in Word Identification    11
Pros and Cons in the Debate    12
What About the Teacher?    12
Again—What About the Teacher?    14

3. THE TEACHING OF PHONICS    16

Early Steps in Word Identification    16
Shortcomings of the Whole-Word Approach    17
Kinds of Word Analysis Possible    17
Readiness for Phonics    18
Initial Instruction in Phonics    19
Classroom Recordings    20
Further Progression in Phonics    30
Generalizations    30

Nature of Generalizations 31
Other Generalizations 32
Letter Combinations 39
Phonics and Syllabification 45
Generalizations About Syllabification 45
Analysis of Multisyllabic Words 47
One Final Comment 50

4. THE PLACE OF PRACTICE 51

5. THE CONTENT OF PHONICS 59

The Simpler Consonants 59
Other Consonants 62
Long and Short Vowels 65
The Letter Y Functioning as a Vowel 67
The Schwa Sound of the Vowels 68
Letter Combinations 68
Consonant Combinations 69
Vowel-Consonant Combinations 70
Consonant-Vowel Combinations 70
Vowel-Vowel Combinations 71
Diphthongs 73
Syllabification 74
Accent 76

6. SOME FINAL COMMENTS ABOUT PHONICS 79

7. LINGUISTICS AND READING 81

What Is Linguistics? 81
Development of Linguistics 82
Linguistics and the Teaching of Reading 83
Linguistic Proposals for Reading 83
Phonology 84
The Proposals of Two Linguists 86
Linguistic Proposals Contrasted with Phonics 90
A Critique of the Linguistic Proposals 94
Possible Contributions of Linguists 98

# PHONICS

*and the*

*Teaching of Reading*

# I

# *Introduction*

Skill in phonics provides one kind of help in identifying written words. It becomes, therefore, a goal to be achieved in elementary school reading programs. To foster such achievement is the purpose of this book. Written for teachers, it is designed to help them with phonics by teaching them more about phonics. It does this by giving attention to (1) the nature of phonics, and of the American English language; (2) the content of phonics; and (3) ways of teaching phonics in the classroom. At the end of the book, a comparison is made between phonics and "linguistic proposals" for teaching reading.

## WHAT IS PHONICS?

Phonics is an adaptation of the highly specialized field known as phonetics. The phonetician, unlike the teacher of reading, concentrates on a study of speech sounds as an end in itself. He is therefore interested in the most subtle variations in sounds, and even in their physiological and acoustical characteristics. He classifies vowels, for example, on the bases of the part of the tongue that acts as articulator; the height to which the tongue is raised when the vowel is sounded; and the shape of the lips in the actual process of sounding.

His classification of consonants also gives attention to articulatory positions. Consequently, certain consonants are referred to as alveolars, *t* and *d*, for example. Other consonants, among them *b* and *p*, are called labials; and still others are known as palatals and include *g* and *k*. In addition, there are voiced and unvoiced consonants, plosives, fricatives, and so on.

Some findings in the phoneticians's classification of speech sounds are highly useful when unfamiliar words are encountered in reading, or when

1

the correct spelling of a word is needed. Others, however, offer no help. Phonics, the particular concern of this book, is the end-product of an attempt to select from the findings of the phonetician whatever is useful for reading and for spelling.* As such, phonics concentrates on the most common sounds in our language, and on the letters or combinations of letters most often used to record them. Attention is given, therefore, to the sounds of long and short vowels, hard and soft consonants, and to the sounds of blends, diphthongs, and digraphs. Because the sounds of letters are sometimes affected by their position in a word, attention is also given to syllabification.

### PHONICS AND THE ENGLISH LANGUAGE

Ideally, at least for purposes of phonics, each symbol or letter in our writing system would represent one speech sound and, in turn, every separate sound would have a single representative symbol. Unfortunately for those learning to read or to spell, this is not the case. Instead, the same sound is represented differently in different words, as in *her, first, word, fur, journey,* and *colonel.* In other instances the same letter, or combination of letters, represents a variety of sounds; for example, the *ea* combination in *clean, bread, break,* and *hearth.* In addition, letters sometimes appear in words but no corresponding sounds occur, as in *debt, have,* and *gnat.*

These kinds of inconsistencies, plus the frequency with which they occur, have led linguists to conclude that of all the great languages in the world, English is the most erratic from a phonetic point of view. But this comes as no surprise to teachers.

### DEVELOPMENT OF THE ENGLISH LANGUAGE

That English has "what is probably the largest body of words ever borrowed by one language from others" partially accounts for the inconsistency so often found between the spelling of a word and its pronunciation [4].† In origin, English descended from the Germanic branch of Indo-European, a long extinct language from which evolved most of the languages now spoken in Europe. As Old English, or Anglo-Saxon, i

---

* Phonics is useful in both spelling and reading. In this book, however, particula emphasis is given to its contribution in the field of reading.

† Figures in brackets apply to references at the end of the respective chapters.

was the dominant language in England from the seventh century to about the middle of the twelfth century. Historians and linguists see the period of Middle English beginning in the twelfth century and extending to the sixteenth, at which time Modern English began to emerge.

Today, many words of high frequency in our language are Anglo-Saxon in origin. Most names of common things (ear, moon, road, water) and for customary actions (eat, wash, work, laugh) are rooted in Old English as are, also, such highly serviceable words as *of, from, there,* and *had.* More specialized words have commonly been borrowed from French, which was particularly influential following the Norman Conquest of England in 1066; and from Greek and Latin, introduced through the literature and writings of scholars. Other but less influential sources of words have been Old Norse (wake, tight), Italian (magazine, bank), Spanish (comply, hurricane), Dutch (filibuster, waffle) and, for American English, the languages of the American Indian (moccasin, woodchuck).

How does this predilection for borrowing words help to account for the inconsistency between spelling and pronunciation so often found in our language? The borrowing of a word, by one language from another, entails the borrowing of its spelling, its meaning, and its pronunciation. Through conscious and careful imitation, the spelling of a word, and also the meaning, can be continued in the second language with relative ease. However, because certain sounds are unique to particular languages, the pronunciation of a word sometimes changes in the borrowing process. This change in spoken language, without a corresponding change in its written representation, results in sounds departing further and further from what a letter, or combination of letters, at first suggested. The end-product is a language in which the spelling of a word is not always a useful guide to its correct pronunciation.

Actually, this lag between changes in spoken language and corresponding changes in written language occurs frequently even when the factor of borrowing is not at work. For example, up until the seventeenth century the *g* in words like *gnat* and *gnarl* was pronounced. After that time the *g* gradually became silent, but its written symbol remained and, obviously, still remains in the spelling of these words [3].

At one time, too, such pairs of words as *sea* and *see,* and *hear* and *here* were pronounced differently and, consequently, were spelled differently [4]. Today we list them under the heading of homonyms, words having the same pronunciation but different spellings and meanings.

Linguists also tell us it was some three hundred years after their pronunciation changed that the spelling of such words as *sun, hour,* and *seem* also changed. Up until that time they continued to be spelled *sunne, houre,* and *seeme* [3]. In many more instances, as in *have, love,* and *cause,* the lag between changes in spoken language and changes in its written representation continues to exist, and continues to cause problems for the child who is learning to read and to spell.

## PRONUNCIATION VARIATIONS IN OUR LANGUAGE

That certain words have more than one "correct" pronunciation is also characteristic of English. In some instances this kind of variation reflects the dialectal quality of language. In other instances the variation relates to grammatical function.

The dialectal element in language is the tendency for people of varying geographical sections of a country to respond differently to identically spelled words. In American speech one of the most striking dialectal differences is in the pronunciation of words that include the letter *r.* In certain sections of the East, for example, *r* seems not to be sounded when it is at the end of a word, or when it precedes another consonant in a word. Yet in these same regions the sound of *r* is inserted at the end of a word when the following word begins with a vowel. Thus, in eastern New England it is common to hear such pronunciations as "hod job" and "vanilla-r ice cream."

Another, and probably the most common kind of dialectal variation is in the pronunciation of vowel sounds. For example, in some sections of our country *rather* rhymes with *father*; in other sections, with *gather.* In some areas the initial sound in words like *on* and *ostrich* is identical, but in other areas *on* begins like *octave* and *October* while *ostrich* begins more like *auto* and *awful.* Other words, such as *forest, calm, roof* and *aunt,* exemplify still more of the differences heard in the pronunciation of vowel sounds.

In addition to these dialectal differences there is still another kind of pronunciation variation—one related to the grammatical function of words. Here, the variation can be illustrated by words like *house* and *rebel,* each of which has two correct pronunciations. Specifically, if *house* appeared in the sentence, "He bought a big house," it would be pronounced one way; but if it were found in the sentence, "That building will house many offices," another pronunciation would be required. So, too, for the word *rebel.* In the sentences "He was a rebel" and "The child did not rebel," its pronunciation varies. And what is correct depends upon the grammatical function of the word in a given sentence. Grammatical function also governs the pronunciation of words like *wind, content, alternate,* and *close.*

## MEANING OF LANGUAGE IRREGULARITIES FOR TEACHERS

What is the relevance, for teachers, of the various characteristics of our language outlined thus far? And, in particular, what is the relevance for those teachers who look to phonics as a source of help in teaching children to read? Essentially, the relevance lies in seeing the nature of our language as defining the value and also the limitations of phonics for reading. That symbols representing speech sounds are used to record our language makes phonic analysis both possible and productive in identifying words. However, the fact that the written representation of our language as a whole shows a highly irregular phonetic system is equally pertinent because it is this that often makes the teaching as well as the use of phonics complicated and even frustrating—and sometimes non-productive. To progress through initial consonant substitution from the known word *care,* for example, to the unknown word *dare* is obviously valuable. Yet when the same principle is employed to arrive at the pronunciation of *dome* on the basis of the known word *come,* the result is anything but helpful. And while it is satisfying for the linguist to see the relationship between the words *debt, doubt,* and *receipt* and their Latin origins *debitum, dubitare,* and *recepta,* it is not at all satisfying for the child who lacks this kind of knowledge, but who still must work out, on his own, the pronunciation of *debt, doubt,* and *receipt*—and, on other occasions, *chamois, limousine,* and *ballet.*

What these problems suggest, then, is that the best use of phonics is a realistic one. And realistically, the use of phonics to identify unfamiliar words in reading sometimes provides their exact pronunciation (plastic, complex); sometimes, a close approximation (chair, formal); and sometimes a misleading combination of sounds (walk, tongue). Consequently, realistic teaching establishes phonics as a *possible* source of help in word identification. It also establishes phonics as a kind of help that functions most successfully when it is used in a flexible trial-and-error way; when the context in which an unfamiliar word appears is used to suggest or to check a pronunciation; and when, in some instances, a dictionary is used to provide help that phonics cannot give because of the nature of the word in question.

## REFERENCES

### FOR TEACHERS

1. Barrows, S. T., *The Teacher's Book of Phonetics*. Boston: Ginn and Company, 1926.
2. Brown, Roger, *Words and Things*. Glencoe, Illinois: The Free Press, 1958.
3. Kenyon, John S., *American Pronunciation; A Text of Phonetics for Students of English*. Ann Arbor, Michigan: George Wahr, 1937.
4. Laird, Charlton, *The Miracle of Language*. Greenwich, Conn.: Fawcett Publications, Inc., 1953.
5. Sapir, Edward, *Language: An Introduction to the Study of Speech*. New York: Harcourt, Brace and Company, 1949.
6. Thomas, Charles K., *An Introduction to the Phonetics of American English*. New York: Ronald Press Co., 1947.
7. Whatmough, Joshua, *Language: A Modern Synthesis*. New York: The New American Library, 1956.

### FOR CHILDREN

The way our language developed presents certain problems for the child who is learning to read and to spell. However, its development also provides a wealth of material for study, and for fun. The following books are recommended as a way of introducing children to interesting aspects of language study.

8. Asimov, Isaac, *Words from the Exodus*. Boston: Houghton Mifflin Company, 1963.
   Describes the origin of frequently used words and phrases that come from the books of Exodus, Leviticus, Numbers, and Deuteronomy. For upper elementary and high school children.

9. Asimov, Isaac, *Words from the Myths*. Boston: Houghton Mifflin Company, 1961.
   Explores Greek myths to discover the origin of words that are a part of our daily language. For children in upper elementary grades and in high school.

10. Barnes, Franklin, *Man and His Records*. Chicago: Follett Publishing Company, 1931.
    Examines, through time, ways in which various languages have been recorded. Includes illustrations.

11. Ege, Otto F., *The Story of the Alphabet*. Baltimore: Norman T. A. Munder and Company, 1921.
Gives an account of each letter of our alphabet. Upper elementary grades.

12. Epstein, Sam and Beryl, *The First Book of Words*. New York: Franklin Watts, 1954.
Gives a simple history of the English language, paying special attention to "interesting" words. Copiously and colorfully illustrated.

13. Ernst, Margaret S., *Words* (3rd Edition, Revised). New York: Alfred A. Knopf, 1957.
Traces the development of the English language. Gives attention, too, to word meanings as they derive from roots, prefixes, and suffixes. Includes a bibliography.

14. Ernst, Margaret S., *More About Words*. New York: Alfred A. Knopf, 1951.
For those "who . . . relish words and their changing histories, who think words are fun." This book gives attention to the histories of certain words. For children in the upper elementary grades and in high school.

15. Funk, Charles E., *Heavens to Betsy!* New York: Harper and Bros., Publishers, 1955.
Describes the sources of curious sayings like "Heavens to Betsy" and "Indian giver." For upper elementary school children.

16. Hays, Elizabeth Le May, *The Tongues of Man*. Chicago: Follett Publishing Company, 1934.
An account of the historical development of language, beginning with the question of who "invented" speech. Illustrated.

17. Laird, H., and Laird, C., *The Tree of Language*. New York: The World Publishing Company, 1957.
Includes information about the beginnings of human language, and of American English. Also includes chapters on the alphabet, English spelling, and histories of individual words. For the upper elementary grades.

18. Lambert, Eloise, *Our Language*. New York: Lothrop, 1955.
Presents a history of English, and also of particular words. Recommended for children in the upper elementary grades and in high school.

19. Ogg, Oscar, *The 26 Letters*. New York: The Thomas Y. Crowell Company, 1956.
An account of the different ways in which man has linguistically expressed himself throughout history. Illustrated. Upper elementary and high school.

20. Pei, Mario, *All About Language*. Philadelphia: Lippincott, 1954.
Deals with language *per se,* then moves on to discuss the English language in particular and other languages in general. Recommended for children in the upper grades of elementary school and in high school.

21. Wiese, Kurt, *You Can Write Chinese*. New York: The Viking Press, 1945.
A pleasant, easy introduction to a writing system different from our own. Charmingly illustrated and easy to read.

# 2

## The Controversial History of Phonics

The teaching of reading has its own history. And at most times during that history some attention has been given to phonics. At most times too, however, the question "Should phonics be taught?" has been asked and conflicting answers have been heard.

### EARLY HISTORY OF PHONICS

In colonial days, best depicted for purposes of this discussion through the *New England Primer,* a child learned to read by first learning the alphabet. As he was warned:

> He who will ne'er learn his ABC
> Forever will a blockhead be.

Once the child mastered the alphabet, he was then required to learn the pronunciation of various lists of syllables by spelling out the letters. On the assumption that the difficulty of learning the pronunciation of letter combinations is directly related to the number of letters combined, shorter syllables came first. Ultimately, words were introduced and, again, the sequence in which they appeared depended upon length and number of syllables.

While the sounds associated with letters received some attention during this colonial period, the spelling out of letters was the principal means used to help children learn to read syllables and, later on, words.

Following the American Revolution the matter of sounds took on new and special importance in reading instruction—in this instance, though, as a way of standardizing American speech. In his well-known *American Spelling Books,* which "taught millions to read and not one to sin," Noah Webster tried to rid the new nation of its dialects by emphasizing, through phonics, a common pronunciation of common words. In reading, the letters of the alphabet were still introduced initially, but now their sounds received special attention. Syllables came next, and they too were organized according to sounds. Once learned, they were followed by lists of phonetically related words.

By 1840 Horace Mann had become a prominent educational leader; and about that time too he was reminding teachers and school administrators it was words that were familiar to young children, and it was letters and letter sounds that were unfamiliar. His reminder, coupled with other reactions against the ABC and sounding methods of teaching reading, led some schools to emphasize a whole-word method. In these instances a child learned to read by first learning whole words.

Later, the researcher Cattell demonstrated through tachistoscopic techniques that a reader reacts to words and groups of words, not to the individual letters within a word. As then interpreted his finding gave further impetus to the whole-word method, and even to sentence and story methods. During these same years, however, texts like the McGuffey and the Beacon Readers were used extensively in the schools, and both emphasized phonics. In some of their stories, for example, vowels in words were diacritically marked, silent letters were crossed out, and identical letter combinations were underlined. Consequently, even while Horace Mann lectured and Cattell worked in his laboratory, much repetition of *nip, nap, nup,* and *sit, bit, rit* was still going on in elementary school classrooms.

## LATER DEVELOPMENTS

About the time of World War I the influence of Gestalt psychology reached educational circles. Its emphasis on the importance of "wholeness" in the learning process tended to discredit still further the phonic methods of teaching reading. So, too, did the exaggerated emphasis given to silent reading during the 1920's. These developments, together with growing interest in less formal and less structured teaching–learning situations, combined to put phonics somewhere in the background as a method of teaching reading. A few writers have said that by 1930 it was dispensed with, but this conclusion seems to be based more on a look at some of the textbooks of the time than on actual classroom observation.

In any case, by 1940 there was an open resurgence of phonics as one aspect of reading instruction. In 1955, however, came Rudolf Flesch's *Why Johnny Can't Read,* which—while indicting the schools for their failure to teach phonics and, consequently, reading—went on to become a best seller. Following *Why Johnny Can't Read* came much counter-criticism, more controversy, and even some "new" phonic systems. Consequently, it is relevant to ask at this point, Where do we now stand in regard to phonics?

### THE CURRENT SCENE

"To be or not to be" is no longer the focus of the phonics debate. Today, the value of phonics for a reading program is generally recognized, if and when it is given an appropriate role to play. What is its "appropriate role," therefore, comes forth as the current question to debate. And, while less dramatic than other questions, it too has been effective in stirring up controversy, and even hot tempers.

Like most debates, this current one has basically two sides. One side sees phonics as *the* method of teaching reading. The other side sees phonics as providing one possible kind of help in identifying new and unknown words. Both positions have certain consequences for classroom practice and both, according to the debaters, have important advantages and disadvantages.

### PHONICS AS *THE* METHOD OF TEACHING READING

When phonics becomes *the* method of teaching reading, certain classroom practices logically follow. For example, phonics will necessarily be introduced at the time reading instruction begins. In this instance, initial instruction takes the form of telling the children the sounds of various letters. Later, these sounds are blended into syllables and then into words.

One well-known phonic system, that of Julie Hay and Charles Wingo [4]—and this, incidentally, was enthusiastically recommended in Flesch's *Why Johnny Can't Read*—begins as follows. Pictures of an apple, elephant, Indian, ostrich, and umbrella introduce the short sounds of the vowels. Ten more pictures, these showing a squirrel, monkey, fox, rabbit, goat, nest, bear, tiger, pig, and dog, illustrate common sounds of the consonants *s, m, f, r, g, n, b, t, p,* and *d.* Once the short vowel sounds and the sounds of these ten consonants are learned they are blended together, first into syllables (su, so, si, se, sa), then into words (sun, sob, sit, set, sat). Following some of these initial blending exercises is a very brief "story" in which, at least for a time, some words are read by the children and some are supplied by the teacher. The very first of these stories is as follows:

> Sam sat in the sun.
> The sun is good for Sam.

While differences are to be found in the various systems that assume phonics to be *the* method of teaching reading, the pattern of Hay and Wingo is fairly typical of the group as a whole. Like the others, it proceeds *deductively*. That is, it begins with generalizations about the sounds of letters which are then applied to the pronunciation of specific syllables and words. Like the other systems, too, that of Hay and Wingo is a *synthetic* process in that it initially concentrates on parts of words which are later combined into whole words.

### PHONICS AS ONE KIND OF HELP IN WORD IDENTIFICATION

When phonics is seen as providing only one possible kind of help in word identification, the sounds associated with letters do not have to be introduced at the time reading instruction begins. Instead, instruction can begin by teaching some words as whole words. In this instance, each word to be learned is presented as a unique and single symbol and the child is expected, in time and with practice, to remember it as such. When enough words have been learned in this way to provide examples of letter-sound relationships, then this is the time when phonics is introduced. Now, recurring parts of known words are used to arrive at generalizations regarding their sounds. For example, when a child knows *my, mother, must,* and *me,* or *big, baby,* and *bunny* he is ready to make generalizations regarding the sounds of the consonants *m* and *b*. And as more words are learned, more generalizations can be made about the sounds associated with other letters and letter combinations.

This particular way of progressing in phonics is often described as an *inductive* and *analytic* procedure. It is inductive because specific words are used to arrive at generalizations regarding the sounds of letters. It is analytic because whole words are analyzed to identify recurring letters and correlated recurring sounds.

## PROS AND CONS IN THE DEBATE

How do the proponents of these two different approaches to phonics substantiate their respective positions? All, it would seem, speak loudest when pointing out disadvantages of the approach that is not theirs. They speak much more briefly, and meekly, when pointing out advantages of their own proposals.

For example, those who see phonics as *the* method of teaching reading usually claim it is only within this framework that phonics is systematically taught; that without a good foundation in phonics, reading problems follow. They also maintain that an approach to phonics which is unlike their own encourages guessing rather than reading, and dependence on the part of the reader rather than the hoped-for independence. They further claim that when children lack independence in working out the pronunciation of unfamiliar words, they are then forced to read dull and senseless texts in which the same words are repeated almost endlessly. The less timid in this group add, still further, that in learning to read whole words "the child grows tired and bored," but that the learning of sounds is "full of fun and adventure." [7]

Like this first group, those in the second—that is, those who look to phonics as providing only one kind of help in word identification—also tend to substantiate their position mainly by pointing out flaws in the approach that is different from their own. They claim, for example, that immediate stress on phonics kills enthusiasm for learning to read and emphasizes pronunciation sometimes to the exclusion of meaning. They would also say that immediate stress on phonics allows for only a deductive approach; and this, in turn, encourages memorization to the exclusion of genuine understanding and insight. Other indictments point to inefficient eye movements, unnecessary lip movements, and slow, laborious reading as unfortunate results of too much phonics too soon.

## WHAT ABOUT THE TEACHER?

In the midst of these counterclaims and countercriticisms, which approach to phonics should the classroom teacher follow? Ideally, findings of carefully thought-out and worked-out research would change the substance of the various arguments from opinion to fact, and thereby would provide direction and justification for classroom practice. Unfortunately, however, existing research in phonics is characterized more by quantity than by quality. And because of the lack of quality, "data" can be found to support almost any claim or any point of view.

Basically, the cause of inferior research in phonics is neither single nor simple. In one sense, however, it can be said to be rooted in inadequate controls. For example, if a researcher examines the value of one method of teaching phonics as opposed to another, both methods ought to be carried out under identical, or at least very closely comparable conditions. Otherwise the researcher would not be justified in attributing differences in outcome or achievement to differences in method. Yet much of the published research in phonics shows little or no attempt to control for teacher-quality or for teacher-motivation. Too often, in fact, the teacher using the "newer method" is a volunteer who, most likely, has considerable enthusiasm for the method he is using, and is therefore much more likely to succeed than the less well motivated teacher— almost regardless of method.

Another related shortcoming in research arises when the researcher assumes controls which do not exist. Many of the earliest studies in phonics, for example, were designed to compare the reading achievement of two matched groups of children, one of which was given instruction in phonics while the other, supposedly, received none. Never taken into account in any of this research was the possibility that children in the so-called "No Phonics Group" actually received instruction in phonics at home or, what is equally possible, had developed their own phonics system. Consequently, what might really have been compared in this research is the reading achievement of children who receive formal classroom instruction in phonics, and the achievement of those who get help in phonics at home or who develop their own system of phonic analysis.

A third kind of weakness in existing research lies in its tendency to examine, as the basis for making comparisons and drawing conclusions, only a limited segment of "reading achievement." Easily testable outcomes such as speed in reading, or ability to call off lists of words have most often been used as the basis for judging the value of some particular approach to phonics. The matter of a child's interest in reading or, perhaps, his ability to read critically or to draw inferences is usually side-stepped. Here, one serious barrier to better research has been the inability to identify specifically all of the skills and reactions that constitute good reading, coupled with the inability to measure adequately some already identified.

One further kind of flaw in the various studies could be attributed to the researcher's tendency to report in only a vague way what he does and what results. Often, for example, a particular "method" is given a label instead of a carefully detailed description. In addition, research findings are sometimes reported "in general" rather than in systematic, quantitative terms. And yet without exactness in research reporting it is impossible to compare meaningfully one study with another, or to cumulate the findings of several similar studies. What results, then, is a long list of small, isolated studies, many of which are devoid of useful findings and of valid generalizations.

What has also resulted, therefore, is a long list of unanswered questions about the teaching of phonics. Still without definite answers are such basic questions as: How much is too much phonics—too much in the sense that it kills interest in reading, impedes its speed, and even obscures the meaning aspect of reading? Is there one sequence for teaching the various phonetic elements that is better than others? Is there a level of intelligence, or perhaps a special kind of intelligence, required for success in phonics? Is this being measured in currently available intelligence tests? What, specifically, can be done to help the child who knows the individual sounds of *b, a,* and *t,* but who seems unable to blend them into the familiar word *bat*?

## AGAIN—WHAT ABOUT THE TEACHER?

At this point the teacher might well be asking, But what about me? I am still expected to make decisions about phonics. What do I do? Where do I begin? What do I do next?

Concerned as he is with immediate problems and responsibilities, the classroom teacher must have at least tentative answers to his questions. Consequently, until good research yields definitive, well-substantiated findings regarding many different aspects of phonics instruction, answers must continue to evolve from personal teaching experience and the teaching experience of others; from extensive classroom observation; from research findings in other areas of learning; and from objective, logical analysis. What follows in Chapter 3, therefore, is an attempt to answer, by means of these various sources, the question of how phonics should be taught in the elementary school classroom.

### REFERENCES

1. Brown, Roger, *Words and Things.* Glencoe, Illinois: The Free Press, 1958.
2. Flesch, Rudolf, *Why Johnny Can't Read.* New York: Harper and Brothers, 1955.
3. Gray, Lillian, and Reese, Dora, *Teaching Children to Read.* New York: Ronald Press Company, 1957.
4. Hay, J., and Wingo, C. E., *Reading With Phonics.* New York: J. B. Lippincott Company, 1948.
5. Kenyon, John S., *American Pronunciation; A Text of Phonetics for Students of English.* Ann Arbor, Michigan: George Wahr, 1937.
6. Smith, Nila B., *American Reading Instruction.* New York: Silver Burdett Company, 1934.
7. Terman, Sibyl, and Walcutt, Charles Child, *Reading: Chaos and Cure.* New York: McGraw-Hill Book Company, Inc., 1958.
8. Thomas, Charles K., *An Introduction to the Phonetics of American English.* New York: Ronald Press Company, 1947.

# 3

## The Teaching of Phonics

Because of the help it offers in word identification, phonics ought to assume importance in any reading program. Yet helping a child to identify words is hardly the same as helping him to read in the full and real sense of the term. To be sure, the good reader *is* skillful in solving the mystery of new and unknown words. But the good reader is also one who knows the purpose for which he is reading, who adjusts his rate of reading to suit this purpose, who evaluates what he reads, who ponders over what he has read, who is able to laugh with one author, analyze with another, and lose himself in phantasy with still another. All of this suggests that instruction in phonics is only one aspect of reading instruction, and that it should not be emphasized to such an extent that equally important components are neglected or omitted.

### EARLY STEPS IN WORD IDENTIFICATION

How should the word identification aspect of a reading program get underway? In the beginning, it is here recommended, instruction ought to focus on whole words rather than on the sounds of parts of words, and for a variety of reasons. In the first place, whole words have meaning and therefore interest for children. They represent things they have seen, people they have known, experiences they have had. They do not, at this stage, represent a blending of individually distinct sounds.

Another factor of importance is that early ability to identify whole words permits the child to do some actual reading quickly. Here, early ability is important because it provides quick reward for the child, meets the expectations he has of school, and allows him to experience reading, from the start, as a way of getting meaning from the printed page. Supplementing this list of reasons for beginning with a whole-word approach

16

is the obvious fact that many of the words immediately needed in any context are highly irregular from a phonetic point of view, words such as *have, the,* and *you.*

## SHORTCOMINGS OF THE WHOLE-WORD APPROACH

To be sure, continuous use of the whole-word approach as the only approach to word identification would have some serious shortcomings. One very undesirable result would be dependency; that is, inability of the child to work out, on his own, the identification of words not yet in his sight-word vocabulary. A second reason for the need, in time, of a more varied approach to word identification is suggested by the way a child often comes to remember whole words. In learning the word *ball,* to cite an example, a child might use the first letter as the significant cue, even though it has been suggested that he "look at the whole word." For him, then, the letter *b* at the beginning of a relatively short word suggests *ball.* In this instance the single, initial letter as a cue is sufficient until he is required to learn words like *but* or *big,* or any other short word that also begins with *b.* Then, what once served as a helpful cue becomes a source of confusion and even error.

In other instances of learning whole words a child might use the general configuration or pattern of a word as the significant cue. In learning *boy* and *funny,* for example, he might come to see those words, and remember them, as particular kinds of patterns formed by particular combinations of letters. These patterns, as cues, are often sufficient until he is also required to learn such words as *toy* and *fancy.* The word *toy,* as a pattern, looks enough like *boy,* and *fancy* looks enough like *funny,* that more confusion can result. And along with the confusion comes the discouragement.

While intelligent use of the context in which a word appears does lessen the problem of cue confusion, the possibility of the problem remains. What it calls for, as did the problem of dependency noted above, is ability in analyzing unfamiliar words in meaningful kinds of ways, and as carefully as is necessary.

## KINDS OF WORD ANALYSIS POSSIBLE

The nature of the American English language suggests the kinds of analysis that are both possible and meaningful. That the language includes such words as *disapprove* and *rerun, playful* and *queenly, unwanted* and *returning* as well as words like *footstep* and *nevertheless* suggests that one kind of analysis possible is structural analysis. Structural analysis, as the name implies, concentrates on the internal structure of words and proceeds in the recognition that (1) certain words in our language are made up of roots combined with prefixes and suffixes, and (2) certain words are made up of two or more other words in combination.

A second kind of word analysis possible is related to the way our language is recorded. It is a kind of analysis, therefore, that is based on sounds associated with letters and combinations of letters. Only this phonic analysis will be considered in the discussion that follows.

### READINESS FOR PHONICS

Acceptance of the whole-word approach as the most meaningful and fruitful way to introduce a child to reading permits use of known words to develop generalizations regarding letter–sound relationships. Consequently, ability to recognize some whole words becomes one component of readiness for phonics. The nature of phonic analysis itself suggests other prerequisites.

It should first be remembered that phonic analysis often provides only an approximate pronunciation of an unknown word. What usually enables the reader to shift from the approximate sound to the exact one is that help or hint which derives from his having the word in question in his listening or speaking vocabulary. For example, if a child were reading the sentence, "The oar fell out of the boat," and the only unfamiliar word were *oar,* phonic analysis could provide a close approximation of its pronunciation. However, if the child knew about oars—perhaps had seen one or had heard stories which referred to one, and thus understood the word *oar* and could meaningfully use the word himself—this background knowledge would bridge the gap between the approximate pronunciation supplied by phonic analysis and the exact one. This kind of language relation suggests that at all grade levels an important part of readiness for phonics is the development of broad listening and speaking vocabularies and, ideally, of a genuine interest in words, since it is the interest that fosters further development.

The nature of phonic analysis also suggests auditory and visual discrimination as other important aspects of readiness for phonics. For example, if a child is to understand inductively that a certain letter, such as *b* in *bag, bell,* and *bunny,* or a certain letter combination, such as *th* in *this, there,* and *the,* records a particular sound, he must first be able to see the common element in the visual representation of each of these groups of words—*b* and *th* in these instances. In addition, he must be able to hear the sounds that are common to their pronunciation. Without these beginnings, a real understanding of letter–sound relationships becomes impossible; and without the understanding, phonics has little meaning for the child.

What about the need to know the names of the letters of the alphabet? Is this too a prerequisite for success in phonics? Here it is important to keep in mind that the names of the letters in our alphabet only rarely suggest the sounds associated with the letters—one notable exception being the names of the vowels, which in fact are the long vowel sounds. As a source of help in identifying correct sounds, therefore, the names of the letters are relatively insignificant. However, as a way of facilitating communication in the teaching–learning situation, knowledge of the names of letters is very significant and, for this reason, ought to be seen as still another kind of readiness for phonics. Just as it would be purposeless, and even ridiculous, for a teacher to refer to one student as "the little girl with the curly hair" and to another as "the boy with the freckles on his nose" rather than to refer to each by name, so too would it be purposeless and ridiculous to have children refer to letters by description rather than by name.

In summary, then, important components of readiness for phonics include a knowledge of the names of letters, ability in auditory and visual discrimination, broad speaking and listening vocabularies, and the ability to recognize some whole words in their written form.

## INITIAL INSTRUCTION IN PHONICS

The particular words that first come to be known in their written form differ from child to child, and from classroom to classroom. Some inevitably will be the highly useful "service words," such as *was, and, they,* and *to.* Others will denote specific persons and specific things, and will have been introduced through a basal reader or a storybook. Still other words will have been learned because of the child's special interest in the person or thing or experience which they represent and recall.

What is relevant for this discussion is that among the early entries in the sight-word vocabulary will be words which can serve as illustrations of certain letter–sound relationships. More specifically, knowledge of words like *my, man, me,* and *must,* or of words like *sand, seven,* and *sit* is useful in identifying sounds of the letters *m* and *s.* At this beginning stage, too, these groups of words serve to introduce what is a new idea for most young children—namely, that the words they have been using and listening to are actually made up of blended but individually distinct sounds; and that these sounds are denoted by particular letters or letter combinations.

In time, the children will also come to see that knowledge of particular letter–sound relationships is useful in progressing, for example, from the known words of *house* and *it* to the pronunciation of unfamiliar words like *mouse* and *sit.* Still later, knowledge of these sounds of *m* and *s,* combined with a knowledge of other letter sounds, and also of factors that affect these sounds, will function in working out the pronunciation of words like *make* and *sing, much* and *safe,* and, still later, *magnificent* and *senile.*

### CLASSROOM RECORDINGS

One kind of progression in phonics, at a very elementary level, is illustrated in a recording made of the work of a first-grade teacher and a group of six children.* In this instance the teacher was attempting to review, and to use, the sound associated with *m.* This sound had been identified by the children earlier in words known to them.

TEACHER.   I'd like you to listen to these words and tell me what's the same about them: *mother, my, mouse.* Did you notice anything about those words that was alike or the same?

STUDENTS.   ———

T.   Listen again, and tell me what's the same about those words: *mother, my, mouse.*

S.   *Mother* and *my.*

---

* This recording and those to follow were made in public school classrooms. No special directions were given to teachers other than the writer's request to record instruction that included phonics. The recordings are not included as models to follow; they are used only for illustrative purposes.

T.   Well, what's the same about *mother* and *my*?

S.   They have the same *m*.

T.   Yes, they begin with *m*. So does *mouse*. So, *mother, my,* and *mouse* all begin with the letter *m* or the *m* sound. Can you tell me some other words that begin with the letter *m*?

S.   *Mother.*

T.   Well, we just said *mother*. What about some others that we didn't just say?

S.   *Must.*

T.   Good. Another?

S.   *Miss.*

T.   Right.

S.   *Baby.*

T.   Well, now, wait a minute. Does that begin with an *m*?

S.   No.

T.   It would have to be *maybe,* not *baby*. It has to begin with an *m*.

S.   *Make.*

T.   That's a good one. Can you think of any others?

S.   ———

T.   Suppose we write those words now. This is the letter *m*. (Writes it on the board.) Now you said *mother, must, mouse*. (Teacher writes each *m* word as she pronounces it.) You see they all have the same starting letter. I have a chart here that has lots of *m* words on it. (Holds up a large chart showing pictures but no words.) Let's look at those (pictures) and see if you can tell me what they are. Now remember, they all begin with *m*. See if Sharon can tell us the first one.

S.   *Monkey.*

T.   Yes. Hear the *m*? The next one?

S.   *Milk.*

T.   Right. Next one?

S.   *Sun.*

T.   Can you make it an *m* word? It looks like a sun, but what could it be that begins with *m*?

S.   *Moon?*

T.   Right. And this?

S.   *Mittens.*

T.   See all the *m* words we didn't think of.

S.   *Monkey.*

T.   Right.

S.   *Mailman.*

T.   Good.

S.   *Balls.*

T.   No, they're not balls. What do you play on the ground? They're smaller than balls, and they begin with an *m*.

S.   *Marbles?*

T.   Right.

S.   *Cake.*

T.   No. Remember, these are all *m* words.

S.   *Steak.*

T.   No, steak doesn't begin with *m*. What's another word for *steak* that begins with *m?*

S.   *Meat.*

T.   Right. Steak is meat. What is this?

S.   *Mailbox.*

T.   Right. And this one?

S.   *Book.*

T.   Is *book* an *m* word?

S.   No.

T.   Well, think of what this could be that begins with *m*. It's like a book, in a way, but it usually has a soft cover. Sometimes we cut pictures out of them.

S.   *Magazine?*

T.   Good. It's *magazine*. What about the last one?

S.   *Music.*

T.   Right. Why do we want to know the sounds of letters? What good is it to know the sounds? How does it help us?

S. 'Cause you learn the words.

T. Yes, it helps us figure out new words. If we know how a word begins it sometimes helps us figure out a new word.

S. When there's an *m,* and then you know what letter that begins with and then you know what you're going to say.

T. Yes, it helps you figure out new words. Let's see if this really works. I'm going to write an old word that you know like this. (Writes *jumps.*) Tell me what that old word is.     *Word that is Known*

S. *Jumps.*

T. Right. Now, watch what I do. I'm going to start that word with an *m* instead of the *j.* Can you tell me what it is?

S. *Mumps.*

T. *Mumps.* Right. You have a new letter, so you have a new word.

S. I had the mumps.

T. How many of you have had the mumps?

S. (Raise hands)

T. Well, anyway you're through with them.

S. I'm through with the chicken pox.

T. (Returning to board) Let's do this again. Watch. How about this word that you all know? (Writes *get.*) ✓

S. *Get.*

T. Right. Now look what I'm going to do. I'm going to take our new sound, and put it in front. Now what word do we have?

S. *Met.*

T. Right, so there's another new word.

The use of a known sound, this time in both initial and final positions, is illustrated in another recording. In this instance the recording was made in a second-grade classroom.

T. I'm going to write some words on the board and I want you to tell me what's the same about the words. (Writes *down, did, do.*)

S. They all begin with the letter *d.*

T. Who can read these words?

S. *Down, did, do.*

T.   Did you hear the beginning sound?

S.   Yes.

T.   Let's see now if we can take that beginning sound and put it on to make a new word. (Writes *town* on board.) What word is this?

S.   *Town.*

T.   What would I get if I took away the *t* and put on the beginning sound you heard in the other words?

S.   *Down.*

T.   Good for you. If we took away the *t* and put a *d* we'd have *down*. Let's look at this word. (Writes *live*.) The word *live*. When something is *live*. This word can be said in two different ways but we're going to look at it as *live*. What would happen if I took away the *l* and put the *d? Live* would then become what? What's that beginning sound? *Live* would become what?

S.   *Dive.*

T.   Good for you. Let's see if we can do another one. Let's see if you can give me some other words that begin with the same sound as *dive, do, did, down.* Can you think of any words that begin exactly the same way as the words I just gave you?

S.   *Die.*

T.   Good. (Writes *die* on board.) Can you think of another?

S.   *Dye.* The one like you dye eggs.

T.   Okay. Yes, we would have that dye. Any other words?

S.   *Didn't.*

T.   What does *didn't* mean?

S.   *Did not.*

T.   Okay. Any others?

S.   *Don't.*

T.   And that means what?

S.   *Do not.*

T.   Can you think of any other?

S.   *Doesn't.*

T.   Now that we know what sound the *d* makes—we've said it in *die, didn't, don't, doesn't*—let's see if we can now use it in a different way. I'm going to give you a word which you all know. (Writes *hat*.) What word is that?

S.   *Hat*.

T.   Now I'm going to change one letter in this word to the letter that we've been working with. Let's see if we can put that *d* sound at the end of the word. (Changes the *t* in *hat* to a *d*.) Can you tell me what the new word is?

S.   *Had*.

T.   Okay. Good for you. Let's see if we can get another one like that. (Writes *sat*.) What word is up there now?

S.   *Sat*.

T.   Let's see if you can tell me what the word is if I change that last letter to a *d*.

S.   *Sad*.

T.   Good for you. Can you tell me any other words that would end with the sound that *d* makes, as in *had* and *sad?*

S.   *Said*.

T.   (Writes *said* on board.) Can you think of any other words that would end with the sound of *d?*

S.   *Mad*.

T.   Good. (Writes it on board.)

S.   *Told*.

T.   Good. We're really hearing our final sounds.

S.   *Showed*.

T.   Good for you. Now I bet many people can get a lot of them from the word *showed* because Richard did something to a word. What did he do?

S.   He put the ending *ed* at the end of *show*.

T.   Yes, and so many can end with that sound. Can you think of another?

S.   *Old*.

T.   Another?

S.   *Shout*. No, *shouted*.

T.   Good, I'm glad you corrected yourself. What would the word *shout* have ended with?

S.   *T*.

T.   And we're looking for the letter *d*, so *shouted* would give us what we want.

Another recording, also made in a second-grade classroom, illustrates another kind of concentration on consonant sounds. In this instance the focus is more complex than the previous one because attention is given to more than one consonant. On the other hand, however, the focus is less involved because the sounds of consonants are only being reviewed; they are not being used to work out the pronunciation of unfamiliar words.

T.   I just put some letters on the blackboard. (Wrote *n, p, s, t.*) Who can read the letters?

S.   *N, p, s, t.*

T.   I'm going to tell you a word, and I want you to listen to the last letter of the word. Then tell me what it is. *His.*

S.   *S.*

T.   Good. *Sleep.*

S.   *P.*

T.   *Pocket.*

S.   *T.*

T.   *Put.*

S.   *T.*

T.   *Pen.*

S.   *M.*

T.   Not *m.*

S.   *N.*

T.   That's right. *As.*

S.   *S.*

T.   *Up.*

S.   *U*—no, *p.*

T.   *Rain.*

S.   *R.*

T.   You're not listening.

S.   *N.*

T.   Here's another word. *Ten.*

S.   *N.*

T.   *Top.*

S.   *T*—no, *p.*

T.   This morning we're going to talk about two other letters. One of them is going to be this letter. (Writes *d.*) The other is this letter. (Writes *m.*) Who can tell me the names of the letters?

S.   *D* and *m.*

T.   I'm going to write two words under the *d,* and I want you to look at them (Writes *doll* and *red.*) What are they?

S.   *Doll* and *red.*

T.   I'm going to write two more under *m.* (Writes *milk* and *him.*) What are they?

S.   *Milk* and *him.*

T.   I'm going to say a word, and I want you to tell me whether you hear a *d* at the beginning, or at the end. *Doll.*

S.   *L.*

T.   You didn't listen to me. I'll repeat it. Is *d* at the beginning or end of *doll?*

S.   Beginning.

T.   Right. James, put a line under the *d* in *doll.*

S.   (Underlines *d.*)

T.   Let's listen to this word. *Red.* Where is that *d* sound, at the beginning or end?

S.   At the end.

T.   Right. Now I'm going to tell you a word and I want you to think whether the *d* is going to come at the beginning or end of the word. Listen. *Said.*

S.   At the end.

T.   Right. (Writes *said* under *red.*) *Head.* Where is it?

S.   At the end.

T.   Right. (Writes *head* under *said.*) *Duck.*

S.   At the beginning.

T.   Good for you. At the beginning of the word. (Writes *duck* under *doll*.) *Day*.

S.   The beginning.

T.   (Writes *day* under *duck*.) *Feed*.

S.   At the end.

T.   (Writes *feed* under *head*.) *Dog*.

S.   At the beginning.

T.   So I'll put it over here. (Writes *dog* under *day*.) Now, who can read all of the words beginning with *d?*

S.   *Doll, red, duck, said.*

T.   Did you listen to what I said? I said read the words where *d* is at the beginning.

S.   *Doll, duck, day, dog.*

T.   Good. Read the words where the *d* is at the end.

S.   *Red, said, head, feed.*

T.   Good.

The practices depicted in these three classroom recordings hardly reflect the most exemplary or inventive kind of teaching. In combination with the discussion presented in the chapter thus far, however, they do point out, and at times imply, certain principles regarding beginning steps in phonics. Each of these principles is listed below, and each is followed by supplementary comments.

1. *The particular sounds initially identified are dependent upon the words that first come to be known.* There is no need for a child to be able to read a given number of words before instruction in phonics begins. The important point is that he is ready for phonics, and that he knows words from which phonetic understandings can be developed.

2. *The first group of words selected to develop phonetic understandings ought to be words that begin with the same consonant.* This criterion for selecting words in the early stages of phonics is defensible because: (1) the sounds of consonants are more singular and more consistent than are the vowel sounds; and (2) the initial sound in a word, as contrasted with the medial and final sounds, is the easiest to identify as an individually distinct sound.

3. *The more words used to illustrate a particular sound, the easier it will be for the child to hear and identify it as a distinct sound.* While a child's sight-word vocabulary is still quite limited, pictures of objects which begin with the sound can serve as further illustrations, providing the pictures portray these objects in a simple, direct way. The difficulty children can have in assigning appropriate names to pictured objects was illustrated in the classroom recordings (*sun* for *moon, balls* for *marbles, steak* for *meat,* and *book* for *magazine*).

4. *The difficulty of identifying sounds common to groups of words varies from child to child.* Often the difficulty does not reflect the nature of the job but rather the newness of it, and even the new kind of language being used. In time, such questions as, Who can think of some other words that sound the same at the end? or What sound do you hear at the beginning of all these words? take on much more meaning and consequently become easier questions to answer.

5. *With different children different kinds and amounts of questioning and prodding are needed to help them arrive at meaningful generalizations regarding letter–sound relationships.* In all cases, however, generalizations ought to evolve from directed learning, not incidental induction. In addition, they should be explicitly stated and, ideally, quickly used.

6. *Identifying sounds of letters is a means toward identifying unfamiliar words.* This identification can sometimes be made by substituting sounds in familiar words, or by adding sounds to them. For example:

FAMILIAR  UNFAMILIAR
WORDS   WORDS

*Consonant Substitutions*

ran ⟶ can
arm ⟶ art
battle ⟶ babble

*Consonant Additions**

car ⟶ cart
and ⟶ band

* Structural analysis is not the concern of this booklet, but it should be pointed out that the most common kinds of additions are structural additions, as: *turn, return;* or *honest, honesty, dishonesty.*

7. *What is presented in phonics at any given grade level depends upon what a child already knows about phonics.* As has been indicated, if the child is just a beginner in phonics—he might be six or eight or even ten years of age—it is best to start with initial consonant sounds. (Bilingual children sometimes have difficulty learning the consonant sounds in American English. In such cases, concentration on initial vowel sounds should probably come first.)

### FURTHER PROGRESSION IN PHONICS

Reference has been made to two factors that influence the sequence in which phonics content is taught: the kinds of words known by the child; and the relative difficulty of the content itself. Actually, however, there is still a third factor. This is the criterion of usefulness. And how useful the various components of phonics will be is what suggests the introduction of vowel sounds even before all of the consonant sounds have been learned.

In phonics the long sounds and short sounds of the vowels get particular attention. This is not to suggest that they are the only sounds recorded by vowels. Rather, it is to see a knowledge of the long and short sounds as establishing a good beginning for skill in phonic analysis.* How far beyond these basic sounds instruction should go is up to the individual teacher but, most of all, is dependent upon the particular children with whom he is working.

For all children the long vowel sounds are relatively simple because, in this instance, the name of the vowel is the long sound of that vowel. In the case of the short vowel sounds, however, some difficulty is commonly encountered because they tend to be kinds of sounds that are difficult to differentiate and to recall. Luckily, many of the words commonly found as early entries in the child's sight-word vocabulary begin with these short vowel sounds; consequently they are "on hand" to serve as examples. These would be words like *ask, end, is, on,* and *up.*

### GENERALIZATIONS

That each of the vowels has two major sounds suggests the need for a child to know the conditions under which each sound predominates. Again, these conditions can be identified inductively, with the help of

---

* More information about the sounds of vowels is included in Chapter 5. That chapter gives detailed attention to the content of phonics.

known words. For example, a child who knows such words as those that follow is ready to identify one kind of condition under which the long sounds of the vowels predominate, and one kind of condition under which short sounds predominate:

|  |  |
|------|------|
| ate  | at   |
| meet | met  |
| rain | ran  |
| pine | pin  |
| bead | bed  |
| cute | cut  |

Ultimately, with the help of words like these and with pertinent teacher-questions about them, the child can be led to see that when a vowel is the only vowel in a word it usually has its short sound; and, secondly, when there are two vowels in a word the first is usually long, and the second silent.

In certain basal readers, the second part of this generalization sounds something like: When two vowels go walking together, the first does the talking and the second does the listening. Actually, the particular wording used to express this or any other generalization in phonics is insignificant. What *is* significant is that the child understands the generalization, and can then use it in his attempt to analyze new words.

### NATURE OF GENERALIZATIONS

Such generalizations as those referred to above can be very helpful in analyzing words—but they are only generalizations, not rules that always work. Our language simply does not allow for absolutely reliable guidelines. Consequently, the generalizations a child comes to know are most useful when he sees them as a starting point in his analysis of a word. And when this word is within a given context, the generalizations become even more useful because the correctness of the "answer" they suggest can be checked against the context in which the word appears. For example, if a child was reading the sentence, "The old man sat down," and the word *old* was unfamiliar, one generalization would suggest that the sound of *o* in *old* is the short sound. (When there is one vowel in a word, that vowel is usually short.) This sound, however, when blended with the sounds of *l* and *d*, says nothing that makes sense about the man referred to in the sentence. Then should follow other possibilities. One possible shift for the child analyzing the word is to try the long sound of *o*. This, when blended with the sounds of *l* and *d*, does make sense. For it does make sense to say, "The old man sat down."

Later on, when words become more difficult, and therefore more difficult to analyze, this use of a context is even more critical and helpful. So too is the trial-and-error approach. Combined—and with generalizations as starting points—they can make a major contribution toward helping a child become a truly independent reader.

### OTHER GENERALIZATIONS

Like the vowels, there are also consonants that have multiple sounds. The letters *c* and *g* can serve as examples here. In this case their sounds are commonly referred to as hard (come, call; go, gate) and soft (city, cent; gentle, giant) sounds. The ultimate aim of instruction centering on these letters is to help children see that *c* and *g* usually have the soft sounds when followed in a syllable by *e, i,* or *y;* and that they most often assume their hard sounds when followed by any other letter.

As with the vowels, the first job is to help the child identify the different sounds of *c* and *g*. This can be done, over a period of time, with selected groups of words. To identify the hard sound of *c,* for example, a group like the following could be used:

| | |
|---|---|
| can | coat |
| cut | came |

Words serving as examples of the soft sound of *c* could include:

| | |
|---|---|
| cent | cinder |
| city | center |

In the same way, the hard sound of *g* could be identified in words like:

| | |
|---|---|
| go | got |
| gate | gave |

Words serving as examples of the soft sound of *g* are usually more advanced. They might include the following:

| | |
|---|---|
| gentle | giant |
| gym | general |

In time, the child ought to be ready to identify the conditions under which each of the two sounds of *c* and *g* predominates. A comparison of lists such as the following could begin to help with this.

|          | gate        |
|----------|-------------|
|          | good        |
| gentle   | ground      |
| general  | glad        |
| giant    | go          |
| ginger   | gum         |
| gym      | grade       |
| gypsy    | game        |
|          | glass       |
|          | grandmother |

It is one thing, of course, to talk about ways of teaching—in this instance the dual sounds of *c* and *g*, and the conditions under which each predominates. Sometimes it is another matter to *do* the teaching. It might be useful, therefore, to return to two more classroom recordings, one of a first grade and the other of a fourth grade.

In the first-grade classroom the teacher was concentrating on the hard sound of *g*. She made no attempt to give it any special name. The purpose was merely to identify the sound.

T.  Children, I'm going to say some words now, and you listen. *Guess, got, girl, gate.* Now you say them after me. *Guess.*

S.  *Guess.*

T.  *Got.*

S.  *Got.*

T.  *Girl.*

S.  *Girl.*

T.  *Gate.*

S.  *Gate.*

T.  Can you tell us something about those words? Just those words, Jeffrey.

S.  They all begin the same.

T.  With what sound do they begin? Do you know the letter?

S.  Yes, *j*.

T.  Oh? Now you listen once again. I'm going to say some more words. You look at me. Watch my lips and listen to what I say. *Good, gave, car, gone*. Who can tell me something about those words?

S.  They all begin—not all, some begin the same.

T.  If you say "some," some must not begin with the same sound. Do you remember what word—or words—did not begin with the same sound?

S.  *Car*.

T.  That's right. Three words began with the same sound. One did not. Do you know what sound those three words began with?

S.  *G*.

T.  Oh, a minute ago we said a *j*. Now which is it?

S.  *G*.

T.  One said *j*. One said *g*. Shall we find out? We know they all begin with the same sound. Now let's see what they look like. Who could repeat the first set of words I gave you? I'll write them on the board.

S.  *Good*.

T.  (Writes *good*.)

S.  *Girl*.

T.  (Writes *girl*).

S.  *Car*.

T.  (Writes *car*.)

S.  *Gave*.

T.  (Writes *gave*.) Now what do you see?

S.  They all begin the same, but one don't begin the same.

T.  Oh, so three begin the same. Let's see how they sound at the beginning.

S.  *Good, girl, car, gave*.

T.  Now what can you tell us about those words?

S.  Three begin the same.

T.  They all begin with what sound?

S.  *G*.

T.  Give the sound.

S.  Guh.

T.  Now we learned these words are the same in two ways. Let's see how well you can recognize words that begin with the *g* sound. I'm going to say some sentences and you listen very carefully and see if you can tell me all the words that begin with this *g* sound. Watch my mouth and listen carefully. The goose walked to the gate.

S.  *Goose* begins with a *g*, and *gate*.

T.  The girl had a gold bracelet.

S.  *Girl* and *bracelet*. No, *gold* and *bracelet*.

T.  Say the *g* words on the board again, and then say *bracelet*.

S.  *Good, girl, gave, bracelet*.

T.  Does *bracelet* begin like the others?

S.  No.

T.  What word does?

S.  *Gold*.

T.  Good girl. Ready for another sentence?

S.  Yes.

T.  Incidentally, I said "Good girl" when Sue answered correctly. What about those two words, "Good girl"?

S.  They begin with the same sound.

T.  Ready for the next sentence? The girl saw the goat.

S.  *Girl* and *goat*.

T.  Let's say those two words.

S.  *Girl, goat*.

T.  Next sentence. The game was given to me.

S.  *Game* and *given*.

T.  I guess we will go home.

S.  *Guess* and *go*.

T.  Good.

The next recording was made in a fourth-grade classroom. In this instance concern was for the two sounds of *c,* and for the conditions under which each sound predominates. Comments about the quality of teaching depicted in this particular recording will be made subsequent to the recording itself.

T.  How many of you have watched your mother bake a cake at home? What would happen if she put in—say four cups of sugar?

S.  It would be too sweet.

T.  And suppose she put in three tablespoons of salt. What would happen?

S.  It might be too salty.

T.  What would it change? Something would change there, wouldn't it?

S.  The taste.

T.  Sometimes I can change words about by doing very strange things to them. Well, not so strange. Really very simple things. Sometimes a sound, like this *c* (writes *c* on board), can be changed around very easily. I'm going to give you the *c,* and it's going to sound two different ways. If I said to you, "I caught a very bad cold, and I had to cough"— there's my word *cough* (writes it on board) with one sound of *c*. And then if I said, "I went for a trip to another city" (writes *city*), here *c* has a different sound. What's the difference in these two sounds of *c*? Is there a letter in the alphabet that sounds like the *c* in *cough?*

S.  *K.*

T.  (Writes *k* above *cough?*) How about the *c* in *city?* Can you think of another letter that sounds like that?

S.  *T.*

T.  No, I think if you think of words that sound like *t* you'll get *talk* and other words like that.

S.  *S.*

T.  Yes, it sounds like *s*. (Writes *s* above *city*.) Now I'm not going to leave these letters here (*k* and *s*) because that would just mix us up. I'm going to substitute another word for this. I'm going to say that if it sounds like the *c* in *cough* then it's a hard *c*. (Crosses out *k* and writes "hard.") And if it has a sound like in *city* it has a soft *c*. (Crosses out *s* and writes "soft.") Let's look at the *o* in cough. Can you tell me what kind of a letter it is?

S.  It's a long letter.

T.  What do we call it? Letters are divided into two parts. Do you remember what they are?

S.  Vowels and consonants.

T.  Who remembers what the vowels are?

S.  *A, e, i, o, u.* And sometimes *y.*

T.  Yes. Let's see if those vowels have anything to do with this *c*. I'm going to say some other words, some words we know from our spelling that have *c* in them, and you tell me whether it has a hard *c* or a soft *c*. *Cold*. Would it be hard, or would it be soft?

S.   It sounds hard.

T.   And so it is. (Writes *cold* under *cough*.) Let me give you another one. *Catch*. Hard or soft?

S.   Hard.

T.   (Whites *catch* under *cold*.) Let me give you another. *Race*.

S.   *R*.

T.   Well, there's an *r* in it at the beginning, but there's a *c* in it. *Race*. Hard or soft?

S.   Soft.

T.   Soft, because it sounds like what?

S.   *C*.

T.   Well, yes, it sounds like the *c* in *city*, like *s*. (Writes *race* under *city*.) I'll give you another. *Face*.

S.   Soft.

T.   Very good. (Writes *face* under *race*.) I'll give you another. *Cake*.

S.   Hard.

T.   Very good. Let me ask you something. I want to know something about this *c*, and about these vowels *a, e, i, o, u*. I wonder if we can see anything about the letter *c* and the vowels in the same word with them.

S.   I know.

T.   Can you see something about the *c* and the vowel in that word?

S.   No.

T.   Look at the words again.

S.   *O* is in *cough*.

T.   Yes.

S.   There's an *i* in *city*.

T.   Yes. Can someone tell me about the *e* in *race*, or in *face*.

S.   You don't hear the *e*.

T.   That's right. It's a silent *e* on the end.

S.   In *face* you don't hear the *e*.

T.   That's right. Is there anything else you can see?

S.   In *city* you don't hear the *y*.

T.   In *city?*

S.   It sounds like an *e*.

T.   Yes, but let's go back to the vowel next to the *c*. In *cough* we have *co*. In *cold* we have *co*. In *cake?*

S.   *Ca*.

T.   In *city?*

S.   *Ci*.

T.   In *race?*

S.   *Ra*.

T.   I want the *c*. There's *c* what? (Points to *race*.)

S.   *Ce*.

T.   In *face?*

S.   *Ce*.

T.   Now there's something I can say about a word that has a *c* and an *o*, and it's the same thing I can say about a word that has a *c* and *a*. Can you tell me what it is? Can you make up a rule from this? If I have a *c* and an *o*, or if I have a *c* and an *a*? What will that do to the sound of *c*?

S.   Make the word harder?

T.   Not the word, but the sound. Can you say that whole thing like I just did?

S.   When you have a *c* and an *o*, and a *c* and an *a*, the *c* makes the word hard.

T.   It makes the sound *c* hard. That's good. How about the next column?

S.   If you have a *c* and an *i*, and a *c* and an *e*, it'll make the *c* soft.

   The importance of carefully choosing those words that are to be used for illustrative purposes is made very obvious by the responses of these fourth-grade children. The first words used—*cough, city, cold, catch*— were consistently appropriate because, in each, *c* was the initial letter and it was followed by a sounded vowel. Notice what happened, however, when the word *race* was selected. Now, as would be expected, the children continued to concentrate on the initial part of the word but in *race* this was not relevant to the discussion. When their attention was redirected, the occurrence of a silent letter at the end of the word was picked up but, again, this was not particularly significant. It led, however, to further concentration on the final letter in a word which, in the case of *city,* was still irrelevant.

Obviously, much of the mental meandering that went on in this discussion could have been avoided had the teacher selected more appropriate words. As it is, the discussion successfully demonstrates that many of the "wrong" responses from children are often reflections of "wrong" questions, and also of poor illustrative material.

## LETTER COMBINATIONS

Recognition that sounds of letters are affected by the particular letter that follows them in a syllable is a kind of preparation for learning that certain letter combinations have their own peculiar sounds. Combinations like *ou* and *ow* are examples of this, but some other combinations would be *au, oo, er, ay,* and *ew.*

In one third-grade class, efforts to teach the sound of *ou* and *ow* went as follows:

T.   Who can name a vowel for me?

S.   *E.*

T.   Okay. (Writes *e* on board.) Another?

S.   *A.*

T.   Okay.

S.   *I.*

T.   Okay.

S.   *U.*

T.   All right.

S.   *O.*

T.   We've discussed when vowels are long—when they say their letter name —and when they are short. But sometimes these vowels are funny. Sometimes they take a friend with them, another vowel or sometimes a consonant, and when they do they're not going to have a short sound and they're not going to have a long sound. Let's see what happens to these words. I'll say them and write them on the board. *Our, cow, out, down.* Who can tell me what's the same about all of these four words I wrote on the board? Listen again. *Our, cow, out, down.*

S.   The *o*.

T.   Yes, the *o* is in all four words, but what sound do we hear in all four words?

S.   *Ou*.

T.   Good. Let's see if you can name some words that have the *ou* sound.

S.   *Now*.

T.   That's a good one. (Writes it under *cow*.) Some other words?

S.   *Bow-wow*.

T.   (Writes it under *now*.) Any others?

S.   ———

T.   Let's use the sound now to learn some new words. (Points to *our*.) What does this word say?

S.   *Our*.

T.   What happens if I add an *s*? (Writes *s* in front of *our*.) What word is that?

S.   *Sour*.

T.   What if I add *fl*?

S.   *Flour*.

T.   (Points to *out*.) What is this word?

S.   *Out*.

T.   What happens if I add *sh*? What is the word?

S.   ———

T.   What's the sound of *sh*?

S.   *Sh*—oh, *shout*.

T.   Good. That's the way we learn new words. Let's see who knows this word. (Adds *sc*.)

S.   ———

T.   This is hard. Who knows it?

S.   *Scout*.

T.   Very good. What's this word? (Points to *down*.)

S.   *Down*.

T.   (Changes *d* to *cl*.) What's this word?

S.   *Clown.*

T.   And if I change it to this? (Changes *cl* to *fr.*)

S.   *Frown.*

T.   What can we say about all of these words? What was the same in all of them?

S.   The *ou* sound.

T.   What makes the *ou* sound? What two letters make the *ou* sound?

S.   *O* and *w.*

T.   Only the *ow?*

S.   *Ur.*

T.   *Ur?* I don't think so. Look at these words again. Look at this word (*our*).

S.   The *ou.*

T.   What can we say about the *ou,* and sometimes say about *ow?* What sound do the *ou* and the *ow* make?

S.   *Ou.*

T.   Yes, they say *ou.* You know a good way to remember that? I'm going to tell you a little story about the *ou* and the *ow.* Sometimes the *o* goes walking with *u* and sometimes it goes walking with *w,* and they look like this. (Writes *ou* and *ow* on the board.) But, you know what happens when the *o* is with the *u,* or it's with the *w*—sometimes with the *w?* A very funny thing happens. The *o* steps on a thorn. What do you think they say?

S.   *Ou.*

T.   *Ou.* Right.

Subsequent to this discussion, the eight children in the group were asked to read the four-line selection "The Owl," then follow the instructions given below it. After finishing the assignment, the group went over it together. (See page 42.)

---

NAME _____

### THE OWL

Ow, ow, the owl bit me.
I found the owl in a tree.
Now I have him in a cage.
He wants to get out.

1. Draw a line under *ou* and *ow* in the story.

2. Read down and across:

| cow | crown | our | out |
|-----|-------|-----|-----|
| now | crowd | sour | shout |
| how | flower | flour | about |
| bow | shower | found | mouth |
| plow | town | ground | house |

3. Finish each sentence by using a word from the list above.
   1. There was a _____ of people in front of the _____.
   2. We get milk from a _____.
   3. Nancy is going to _____ to buy some _____.
   4. The king wears a _____ on his head.

---

A teacher of a fifth-grade class focused her instruction on the combination of *a, r,* and *e* as heard in the word *dare*. She was a new teacher, and this might account for the way her instruction proceeded.

T. We've been working on the sounds of different vowels. Yesterday we worked on the sound of *e*. And we had a long *e* sound like in *me*. Who can give me another word with a long *e* sound?

S. *See.*

T. Very good. And the short *e* sound was *ĕ*, and we used the word *get*. Who can give me another word with a short *e*?

S. *Electric.*

T. Very good. Today we're going to work with the *a*. And for the long *a* we have the sound as in *name*. (Writes *name* on board.) Can anyone think of another word with a long *a?*

S.  *Same.*

T.  *Same.* That's right. (Writes *same* under *name.*) Another?
Students supply the words *game, frame, blame, flame, came, tame* and teacher writes each one on the board as a child pronounces it.

T.  I want you to look very carefully at these words. Aside from the fact that they all have a long *a*, they all have something else that's the same.

S.  *A, m, e.*

T.  They all end in *e*. These all happen to end in *ame* because they all rhyme. But they all end in *e*. I want you to keep that in mind. Now we have the sound of the short *a*, and that sound is *ă*, as in *man*. (Writes *man* on the board.) Can you think of a word?

S.  *Hand.*

T.  Very good. (Writes *hand* under *man.*)
Students call out the words *mat, dance, jam*, the name *Sam*, and *can*, and teacher writes each one on the board.

T.  You learned earlier that you could always tell a long *a* if the word ended with an *e*. If you had a word with an *e* we were always told that the vowel would always be a long *a*. I'm going to show you something. (Writes *dare* on board.) Who can say that word for me?

S.  *Dare.*

T.  Here you have an *a*, and your word ends in an *e*, but this is not the sound of the long *a*, is it? So we see that that rule that we learned a long time ago isn't true. Can you think of some other words that end in *e*, and that have the vowel *a* but that have the sound like in *dare?*

S.  *Bare.*

T.  (Writes *bare* under *dare.*)

S.  *Care.*

T.  (Writes *care.*)

S.  *Air.*

T.  (Writes *air.*)

S.  *Hair.*

T.  All right. (Writes *hair.*)

S.  *Chair.*

T.  (Writes *chair.*) One more?

S. *Pair.*

T. (Writes *pair.*)

Immediately following this discussion, a page in a workbook was assigned to the group of seven children. The page was concerned with the three sounds of *a* as heard in *ate, ask,* and *care.*

In this particular lesson enough things went wrong to warrant a detailed analysis of it. The comments enumerated below follow the sequence of the lesson itself.

1. For her purposes the teacher obviously wanted to make use of words in which there were two vowels, the first of which was a long *a,* and the second a final *e.* However, she phrased her question, "Can anyone think of another word with a long *a?*" Luckily the children followed her example of *name* with words like *came, blame,* and *tame,* yet in answer to the question posed they might have given such words as *sail, rain,* and *pay.* These would hardly have been what the teacher wanted, but they would have represented correct responses to her question.

2. That all of the examples given had *ame* in common obscured the fact that all of them also ended in *e.* Because of this, the teacher answered her own question about the similarity of the words being discussed.

Actually, when a new idea is introduced, it is often helpful if the teacher herself selects words to illustrate the point of the instruction. This controls the focus, but it also simplifies it at a time when simplicity is most vital. And later on there will be many opportunities for the children to supply other examples. Almost inevitably their examples will open up areas for discussion. This happened in the lesson being analyzed when the children responded with the words *air, hair, chair,* and *pair.* In this instance, however, the examples were simply passed by.

3. Words that rhyme end with the same sound, but not necessarily with the same letters. *Name, same,* and *game* rhyme, but so do *kite* and *night,* and *go* and *though.*

4. It would seem that this teacher discussed the short sound of *a* only because it appeared on the workbook page to be assigned. However, the group of children seemed to know the sound, and probably no further practice was needed at this time.

5. The teacher's comment, "If you had a word with an *a* in it, and the

word ended with an *e,* we were always told that that vowel would always be a long *a,*" shows little understanding of the nature of phonic generalizations. Her subsequent comment, "So we see that rule that we learned a long time ago is not true," shows even less understanding—or maybe just a poor choice of words. In any case, both teachers and children ought to see and use phonic generalizations as guidelines and starting points, not as "rules."

## PHONICS AND SYLLABIFICATION

Words chosen to illustrate various points made throughout this chapter have been relatively simple kinds of words. In addition they have usually been words of one syllable. As monosyllabic words, however, they were unable to demonstrate an essential characteristic of letter–sound generalizations for our language. They would not demonstrate, for example, that the three-letter combination of *a, r,* and *e* usually sounds as it does in *dare* when the three letters are *within the same syllable* of a word, but that each has its own sound when they appear in different syllables (a-re-na). Nor would monosyllabic words demonstrate that the letter combination *aw* has a particular sound when it is *within the same syllable* (aw-ful), but that each letter has its own sound when appearing in separate syllables (a-way).

An essential characteristic of letter–sound generalizations, then, is that they are based on the syllable, not on the word. In the case of monosyllabic words this distinction obviously is unnecessary. In the case of multisyllabic words, however, the distinction is vital and must be made.

### GENERALIZATIONS ABOUT SYLLABIFICATION

With the syllable as the pronunciation unit, phonic analysis of a totally unfamiliar word begins with a division of the word into syllables. Once the division is made, each syllable can be analyzed and then the syllables can be blended into the word itself.

How is this division made? Within the written form of a word there are certain visual cues that suggest correct syllabification. Statements about these cues are other generalizations that are important for phonics.* One generalization, for example, is: Every syllable must have a

---

\* Generalizations regarding syllabification are included in Chapter 5.

sounded vowel. This immediately suggests that words like the following could only be words of one syllable:

| | | |
|---|---|---|
| brisk | self | month |
| smash | rich | splotch |

Another generalization might be stated as: When two consonants appear between two vowels, a syllable division is usually made between the consonants. This particular generalization is helpful in analyzing words like:

| | | |
|---|---|---|
| ac cent | dis may | cir cum vent |
| num ber | pur port | el der ber ry |

Another very useful generalization about syllabification suggests: When a single consonant appears between two vowels, the consonant is usually in the same syllable as the vowel following it. This generalization, together with the one just cited, would function in the syllabic division of the following words:

| | | |
|---|---|---|
| re pub lic | cru ci fy | con vo ca tion |
| ar gu ment | gar ri son | in de pen dent |

In discussing these various generalizations with students it is important to point out to them that the syllabic division of a word suggested by the generalizations will not always be identical to the syllabification given in a dictionary. The word *independent,* for example, appears as *in de- pend ent* in a dictionary, but as *in de pen dent* on the basis of a generalization cited above. The reason for discrepancies is that the dictionary preserves the integrity of the root word, while the generalizations in phonics are to help with correct pronunciation.

*Arriving at These Generalizations*

Like the generalizations about sounds of letters, those concerned with the division of words into syllables can be arrived at inductively, with the help of known words. The generalization about dividing a word between consonants, for example, could come from such relatively simple words as those listed at the top of page 47.

|        |         |          |
|--------|---------|----------|
| un der | hel lo  | bas ket  |
| hap pen| num ber | cap tain |

The syllabic generalization about the single consonant preceded and followed by vowels could be arrived at through careful inspection of words like:

|        |       |         |
|--------|-------|---------|
| a way  | a go  | e lect  |
| be gin | so da | lo cal  |

In this way, then, generalizations about syllabification accumulate gradually. And, combined with the generalizations about sounds, they provide the child with important skills for analyzing words of more than one syllable.

## ANALYSIS OF MULTISYLLABIC WORDS

Sometimes the pronunciation of unfamiliar multisyllabic words can be achieved through their relationship to words already known. For example:

| FAMILIAR WORDS | UNFAMILIAR WORDS |
|----------------|------------------|

*Letter Additions*

| able  | ⟶ | stable |
|-------|---|--------|
| over  | ⟶ | overt  |

*Letter Substitutions*

| battle | ⟶ | babble |
|--------|---|--------|
| ramble | ⟶ | rumble |

In other instances, the unknown word will have to be analyzed in a letter-by-letter fashion. For example, let us suppose a child came across the three sentences below, and the words in italics were unfamiliar to him:

1. The heated *argument* went on for more than an hour.
2. His grandmother is quite *senile*.
3. The scientist was testing his *hypothesis* in the laboratory.

How would the child go about analyzing these three words? Were he "thinking out loud" and in a very explicitly detailed way, his thoughts might sound as follows:

### Argument

This word probably divides between the *r* and the *g*, and between the *u* and the *m*. That gives me:

ar    gu    ment

An *r* following a vowel in the same syllable affects the sound of the vowel, so *ar* probably sounds the way it does in *car*. In the syllable *gu* there's only one vowel, but it comes at the end of a syllable so this *u* probably has its long sound. When *g* is followed by *u* it generally has its hard sound. So, long *u* says *ū*, and *gu* says *gū*. That takes care of that syllable. Now for *ment*. Oh, I know that. It says *mĕnt*. I've seen that in words like *basement* and *statement*. I know the word. It's *argument*—"The heated argument went on for more than an hour."

### Senile

In this word the *n* probably joins with the *i* to make the syllable *nile*. Maybe *nile* sounds the way *pile* does. With *se*, the *e* is probably long because it's the only vowel, and it comes at the end of the syllable. So long *e* says *ē*, and *se* would be *sē*. *Sē-nīle*. I wonder if that's correct. I've never heard of the word *senile*. I wonder what it means. Maybe I had better look in a dictionary. Let's see. Oh, here it is. It does say *sē-nīle*, and it means, "of old age." "His grandmother is quite senile." That makes sense.

### Hypothesis

In this word *y* is probably acting like a vowel, so then *y* would go with the first *h*, and the *p* would go with the *o*. *T* and *h* usually stay together and the *s* would go with the *i*, so that means the word probably looks like:

hy    po    the    sis

Let's see. If *y* is like a vowel here, it probably has a long vowel sound, probably like a long *i*. So, *y* says *ī*, and *hy* sounds like *high*. In *po* the *o* is at the end of the syllable, so it probably has its long sound. And, long *o* says *ō*, so *po* would say *pō*. I wonder if *t, h,* and *e* sound the way way they usually do. Maybe not. Maybe the *e* has its long sound; it's at the end of that syllable. So, long *e* would say *ē*, and *the* would say *thē*. *Sis* I know. It says *sĭs*. Now let's put all of this together. Hȳ-pō-thē-sĭs? "The scientist was testing his hypothesis in the lab." I wonder what that means. Maybe I had better look it up in the dictionary. Here it is. Oh, it's hȳ-pŏth-ə-sĭs, and it means "Something not proved, a theory." Sure. "The scientist was testing his hypothesis in the laboratory."

A close look at the thinking of this child shows it is the end-product of many different learnings and experiences. Analyzed, his procedure in working out the pronunciation of the words reveals pertinent techniques, most of which are appropriate for words of one or more than one syllable. Each is made explicit below:

1. Phonic analysis of a totally unfamiliar word begins by dividing the word into syllables. Each syllable is then separately analyzed.

2. Analysis of each syllable requires use of generalizations about the sounds of single letters, and letter combinations; and also about the effect of the position of a letter in a syllable on its sound.

3. When a syllable begins with a consonant followed by a vowel (*gu* in *argument; se* in *senile*), the vowel is sounded first and is then blended with the sound of the consonant. In all other instances, blending proceeds in the order in which letters appear in the syllable.

Beginning the analysis of a syllable with a vowel, even though the vowel is preceded in the syllable by a consonant, avoids a common kind of blending problem. This problem grows out of the "impurity" of the sounds of consonants when these consonants are sounded in isolation. For example, the hard sound of *g* in isolation is most accurately represented by *g* plus the sound of a short *u;* or, as is the practice, its sound would be spelled *guh*. Consequently, a phonic analysis of the syllable *gu* which began with the sound of *g* might interject into the syllable a superfluous vowel sound. When, to the contrary, analysis begins with the sound of long *u*, and moves from this to the sound of *gū*, the blended sound resulting is like the sound of the syllable as it is actually heard in the word *argument*.

The importance of this way of proceeding is seen in the child who, for example, knows the individual sounds of *b, a,* and *t,* but cannot seem to blend them into the familiar word *bat*. What he hears, very often, is a combination of *bu-a-t* which, for him, does not suggest *bat*. Better to proceed as:

$$\breve{a} \longrightarrow b\text{-}\breve{a} \longrightarrow b\text{-}\breve{a}\text{-}t$$

than as

$$b(u) \longrightarrow b(u)\text{-}\breve{a} \longrightarrow b(u)\text{-}\breve{a}\text{-}t.$$

4. The sounds of some syllables can be recognized on the basis of their relationship to known words, or to parts of known words. Recognition of relationships functioned with *ment* in *argument; nile* in *senile;* and *sis* in *hypothesis.*

5. Generalizations about sounds and about syllabification are most productive when the word in question is unknown only its written form. For example, if the child referred to above had previously heard the word *hypothesis,* or perhaps even knew it well enough to use it in his own conversation, then his skill in phonics, combined with his knowing the word in its spoken form, would probably be sufficient to help him identify the word the first time he encountered it in written form.

### ONE FINAL COMMENT

This chapter on "The Teaching of Phonics" has given attention to generalizations about sounds of letters, and about syllabification. In particular, it has shown how understanding and flexible use of these generalizations contribute to independence in reading unfamiliar words. Such concentration, however, was not designed to overshadow the many words in our language which are sufficiently irregular, from a phonetic point of view, to render analysis of them relatively useless. At an elementary level these would include words like *was* and *talk;* at a more advanced level, words like *aisle* and *chamois.*

Mention of this now is not to put a pin into the phonics balloon. Rather, it is to end the chapter on a realistic level, and to put phonics into a realistic setting. Phonics is useful, phonics is important, phonics is necessary in a really good reading program. Yet there will always be times when some words must be taught as whole words, and this need will occur at all grade levels. To recognize this is to recognize the nature of our language and of phonics.

# 4

## The Place of Practice

Ability in reading comprises (1) motor skills, (2) arbitrary associations and understandings, and (3) comprehension. While comprehension—whether of a word, a paragraph, an inference, or whatever—is of the very essence of reading, comprehension is still dependent upon proficiency in certain motor skills, and upon the understanding and recollection of some arbitrary procedures and associations.

In the area of motor skills, for example, good reading includes efficient eye movements and the ability to focus on a given word, or line, or even page. In what might be categorized as the "arbitrary elements," successful reading requires cognizance of the top-to-bottom and left-to-right direction of our written language, and it also requires identification and recollection of the symbols used to record it.

It is to this identification and recollection process that phonics makes its contribution. By concentrating on associations existing between letters and sounds, phonics helps to identify unknown words and to recall those that are somewhat familiar.

Establishing associations, in any area, is a kind of learning that is promoted and sustained by practice. Only rarely are associations permanently fixed following one response to a particular stimulus. In phonics, for example, a correct but single response to the sound of a letter or letter combination is usually not sufficient to establish that response in the learner. Instead, correct and repeated responses are generally necessary. This suggests, then, that if a really effective job is to be done in phonics, teachers must provide children with opportunities for practice in the various phonic skills. And, ideally, for a kind of practice that is of the highest quality.

Practice of high quality can be characterized first of all in terms of function. Here practice is seen as (1) reviewing and extending the learner's comprehension of what is being fixed, and (2) making permanent and useful what is comprehended.

A second way of depicting effective practice is to note the various elements that comprise it. Because these elements have specific implications for teaching, they will be discussed in some detail. Five general statements about practice will be made, each to be followed by additional comments.

1. *Practice ought to concentrate on a deficiency.* Never is practice for the sake of practice. Rather, it is for learning, improving, or perfecting a skill. Yet aren't children sometimes required to go over again and again —and sometimes still again—what they already know and are able to use? Were the basic causes of this needless repetition sought, one would undoubtedly be found in misuse of material that was designed for children in general. Here, phonics workbooks must get attention.

The primary purpose of a workbook is to provide practice. Most workbooks cover a wide variety of skills that children in general will probably need to learn. But what teacher works with children in general? Instead, isn't he teaching Sue, who just can't remember the short vowel sounds; and Lee, who seems content to call any word by any name; and Bob, who learns everything almost instantaneously; and Arlene, who can repeat all of the generalizations in phonics but is unable to use any of them?

This wide range of abilities in a classroom is typical; it is not exaggerated or manufactured. It is what presents constant challenge to the sensitive teacher who tries to meet it in the way he organizes a classroom for instruction.

Essentially, good classroom organization is a way of working with children that allows the teacher to individualize his instruction to the greatest degree possible. No magic or single formula achieves it. With a new teacher who is also a conscientious and sensitive person, appropriate organization gradually evolves. With a more experienced teacher, the "formula" is shifting and changing from time to time, and from class to class. But with both, working with small groups of children, and sometimes with individual children, is a "must." Within this organizational framework, then, the way is paved for instruction that is truly enlightening; for the use of materials—and these might include workbooks—that are challenging but not frustrating; and for practice that is needed.

2. *The situation in which a skill is practiced ought to be typical of the one in which the skill is to function.* Only rarely, in his reading, will a child be required to use phonic skills on a word in isolation. Most often, an unfamiliar word will be part of a context that might be as short as a phrase or as long as a book. Ideally, then, school practice in phonics ought to be heavily weighted with opportunities for using the skills of phonics on words within a context. More specifically, if a child knows the word *call,* and also knows the sounds of *h* and *t,* the most realistic practice in using what he knows will not be fostered in responding to:

> call
> hall
> tall

but, rather, in the reading of:

> I will *call* you.
> Our phone is in the *hall*.
> One has to be *tall* to get to it.

To be sure, none of this suggests there is never the need to isolate certain words, or certain sounds, or certain generalizations—whatever the case may be—for special emphasis and concentration. There will certainly be occasions when words like *was* and *saw,* or *accept* and *except,* or *thought, though,* and *although* need to be put side-by-side—or preferably one under the other—to point out striking similarities and important differences. At other times a problem may arise that calls for repeated use of one particular generalization, and this is often expedited when practice is focused on a selected list of words rather than on sentences or an integrated paragraph. In general, though, practice on a skill should be of a kind that closely resembles the way the skill will be used. And in phonics, use is with words in context.

3. *Practice, by its very nature, involves repetition. However, ideal practice involves thoughtful and attentive repetition.* The story of the child who, because of poor grammatical habits, was kept after school to write one hundred times, "I have gone" becomes relevant here, especially

when the end of the story is also told. For, having done the job assigned, the child left his neatly written paper on the teacher's desk with the following postscript: "I did my work. I have went home."

The lack of progress evident in the postscript should not be surprising when the nature of the assignment is considered. To be sure, the assignment did allow for repetition, but hardly for a kind of repetition that demanded thoughtful responses. It is very likely, in fact, that the child mechanically repeated *I* one hundred times, then *have,* and then *gone.* At no time, possibly, did he actually repeat the combination *I have gone.*

In addition, the amount of repetition required by the assignment was excessive. To do a basically uninteresting job one hundred times is hardly to encourage proficiency. Rather, it is to encourage careless and even wrong responses, and certainly distractions.

Unfortunately, in phonics too, assignments are sometimes made that call for responses of a mechanical kind, and for repetition that becomes a burden. Witness the following:

### THIRD GRADE TEACHER

Listed on the board are thirty-five words. I want you to rewrite them in two columns. Fold your paper so that you have two columns, and in one write all of these words that have just one vowel, and in the other all of the words that have two vowels.

*Comment:* Basically, this assignment calls for counting vowels and copying words—too many words for third-grade children. Both are very mechanical kinds of responses, and neither contributes very much to skill in phonics.

### FIFTH GRADE TEACHER

I've given you a sheet that has about 25 words on it. Look up each one in your dictionary, and write in the diacritical marks that you find in the dictionary for each word. Be sure to include all of them.

*Comment:* Looking up some twenty-five words in a dictionary is a monotonous task. And by this time, the matter of "looking up words" should be an accomplished skill. In addition, diacritical marks need to be interpreted only, not duplicated. Consequently, this copying assignment seems quite purposeless.

## Sixth Grade Teacher

Turn to the page in your dictionary where words beginning with *c* start. Go through the list and copy only those that begin with the soft *c* sound. Find as many as you can, and don't skip over any.

*Comment:* This assignment does provide practice in identifying one of the common sounds of *c*—but perhaps too much practice. In the dictionaries used by this group of sixth graders there were 108 words beginning with the soft *c* sound. In this instance, finding "as many as you can" was quite an extensive job, and after a while not a very compelling one.*

4. *Practice, especially in the early stages of learning, should be supervised.* One possible response to this recommendation might be, "But I don't have time. I have a class of thirty-seven children!" Unfortunately, the idea of supervision has come to be equated with a teacher hovering over a child as he works at his desk. It is not within this context, however, that the above suggestion is made. Instead, supervision is intended to include any guidance a child is given to help him see either the correctness or the error of his responses. Why is this guidance important? And who is available to give it?

The responses a child makes are the responses he learns. If he repeatedly responds to the word *father,* for instance, with the sound recorded by the letters *d, a, d, d, y,* then what he is learning is an incorrect response. Or, to cite another example, if he is asked to make out a list of words that include the soft *g* sound, and what he selects are words like *gun, grind, again,* and *gallon,* then what he is learning—unless his responses are checked and changed—is an incorrect understanding of the soft sound of *g.*

Obviously, then, guidance is of great importance. But, it might be asked, Who or what is to provide the checking and the guidance? Sometimes the teacher, sometimes the children themselves with the help of the teacher, and sometimes the materials being used.

Ideally, most guidance would come from the teacher as he worked

* References listed at the end of the chapter give suggestions for assignments in phonics. Not all of the assignments are of the highest quality, so it is hoped that selections will be made on the basis of the criteria for good practice discussed in this chapter.

with individual children. Not because the teacher is one who has all of the answers, but because he is another *person* to whom the child can respond, pose questions, make comments, and so on. And there will be many instances when a teacher can give individual guidance. There will be many other times, however, when he must guide the responses of children in groups. Here, two procedures are commonly followed. With the help of the teacher (1) each child corrects his own work, or (2) each child corrects the work of another child in the group. What is happening in each of these two situations?

In the first, each child is finding out which of his responses was correct, which "went astray," and why they went astray. This ought to provide direction for new and better responses. In the second situation, each child is finding out what another child does or does not know; he is finding out far less about what he himself knows or what he still needs to learn. Since one of the purposes of practice is to learn about one's own deficiencies, not those of others, the first situation is obviously far better than the second.

One further kind of guidance during and following practice sessions is also available to the child. This is to be found in materials often called "self-instructional."* In these, explanations or reviews of some new learning are made, directions for practice are given, and answers are provided. The aim of the material is twofold: to supplement instruction of the teacher, and to help the child become an independent worker and learner. While more and more material of this nature is being published, it is a kind that can be made in a simple form by the teacher himself. The obvious advantage of this, of course, is that the teacher knows the child, and therefore knows what he still needs to learn and to practice.

5. *Recognition of accomplishment should grow out of practice sessions.* Practice, it has been said, is for learning, or improving, or perfecting a skill. It assumes some kind of deficiency, therefore, and it anticipates some measure of accomplishment. What is *not* accomplished by any given practice suggests to the teacher the direction and content of future practice. But what *is* accomplished becomes the opportunity for the learner to experience success and, in turn, encouragement. The

* See, for example, *Ways to Read Words* (Bureau of Publications, Teachers College, Columbia University) and *Word-Analysis Practice* (Harcourt, Brace, and World, Inc.).

positive outcome of practice, therefore, should be made both possible and visible.

Genuine success becomes possible when practice allows for concentration on a deficiency, and also for some improvement in it. This means that the content of practice should never be so simple that it bores and wastes time, or so difficult that it frustrates and discourages. Instead, somewhere "in the middle" is the assignment in which there is room for success and for learning too.

But what is the value of success that remains hidden and unnoticed? And who has more opportunity than the teacher to let it "rise and shine"? Fortunately, teachers in classrooms all over the country are taking advantage of their opportunity by the positive comments they make, by the encouraging notes they take time to write on children's papers— even by the approval in their eyes and the smiles on their faces. For these are the teachers who *know* that nothing succeeds better than success itself.

## REFERENCES

1. Bond, Guy, and Tinker, Miles A. *Reading Difficulties*. New York: Appleton-Century-Crofts, Inc., 1951, Chapter 12.
2. Darrow, H. F., and Van Allen, R. *Independent Activities for Creative Learning*. New York: Bureau of Publications, Teachers College, Columbia University, 1961.
3. Deboer, John J., and Dallmann, Martha. *The Teaching of Reading*. New York: Henry Holt and Company, 1960, Chapter 6B.
4. Dechant, E. V. *Improving the Teaching of Reading*. Englewood Cliffs, New Jersey: Prentice-Hall, Inc., 1964, Chapters 10, 11.
5. Durrell, Donald D. *Improving Reading Instruction*. Yonkers-on-Hudson, New York: World Book Company, 1957, Chapters 11, 12.
6. Feldmann, S. C., and Merrill, K. K. *Ways to Read Words*. New York: Bureau of Publications, Teachers College, Columbia University, 1959.
7. ———. *More Ways to Read Words*. New York: Bureau of Publications, Teachers College, Columbia University, 1959.
8. Gray, Lillian, and Reese, Dora. *Teaching Children to Read*. New York: The Ronald Press Company, 1957, Chapter 11.
9. Gray, William S. *On Their Own in Reading*. Chicago: Scott, Foresman and Company, 1948, Chapters 10-13.
10. Harris, Albert J. *How to Increase Reading Ability*. New York: Longmans, Green and Company, 1956, Chapter 14.
11. Hester, Kathleen B. *Teaching Every Child to Read*. New York: Harper and Brothers, 1955, Chapter 11.
12. Hildreth, Gertrude. *Teaching Reading*. New York: Henry Holt and Company, 1958, Chapter 15.

13. McKim, Margaret G. *Guiding Growth in Reading.* New York: The Macmillan Company, 1955, Chapter 9.
14. Miel, Alice (Ed.) *Individualizing Reading Practices.* New York: Bureau of Publications, Teachers College, Columbia University, 1958, Chapter 5.
15. Russell, David H., and Karp, Etta E. *Reading Aids Through the Grades.* New York: Bureau of Publications, Teachers College, Columbia University, 1955.
16. Smith, Nila B. *Reading Instruction for Today's Children.* Englewood Cliffs, New Jersey: Prentice-Hall, Inc., 1963, Chapter 21.

# 5

## The Content of Phonics

The third chapter in this book focused on the teaching of phonics. In doing so, it gave only incidental attention to some of the content of phonics—for example, the hard and soft sounds of *c* and *g,* and the long and short sounds of the vowels. The purpose of this fifth chapter is to review that content in detail, and in a way that will provide teachers with reference material.* The review proceeds by covering five topics, in the following order: (1) Consonants; (2) Vowels; (3) Letter Combinations; (4) Syllabification; and (5) Accent.

### THE SIMPLER CONSONANTS

Probably the quickest way to identify the consonants is to say they are all of the letters in the alphabet except the vowels, and the vowels are *a, e, i, o,* and *u.* As compared with these vowels, the consonants are relatively consistent in the sounds they record. This is especially true of *b, f, h, j, k, l, m, n, p, r, t, v, w, y,* and *z,* which nearly always record the sounds heard in the initial part of the following words:

| | | |
|---|---|---|
| *b*at | *l*ike | *t*oy |
| *f*un | *m*uch | *v*ery |
| *h*ow | *n*ot | *w*ay |
| *j*am | *p*an | *y*es |
| *k*ite | *r*un | *z*oo |

* *A Phonics Test for Teachers,* by Dolores Durkin (Bureau of Publications, Teachers College, Columbia University), can be used in reading methods courses to find out what teachers and student teachers know about the content of phonics. The test is designed to instruct as well as to diagnose.

Even in the case of these fifteen consonants, however, there are instances when they are silent, and when they combine with other letters to record other sounds. Instances when they commonly have no phonetic value will be pointed out here. Comments about the sounds they record in combination with other letters will be found under the topic of Letter Combinations.

## B

When *b* follows *m* in a word, and is in the same syllable, it is silent.

climb                                   dumb

When *b* precedes *t* in a syllable, it is silent.

debt                                    doubt

## H

When *h* is the first letter in a word it most often sounds as it does in *he,* but it is sometimes silent.

heir                                    hour

Whether an initial *h* is sounded or is silent depends upon whether the word in question was absorbed into our language directly from Latin, or from Old French. If of Latin origin the *h* is sounded; if from Old French, it is silent.

Other examples of *h* as a silent letter are cited below:

The letter *h* is silent when it follows *g* at the beginning of a word.

ghost                                   ghetto

The letter *h* is silent when it follows *k* at the beginning of a word.

khan                                    khaki

The letter *h* is silent when it follows *r* at the beginning of a word.

　　　rhetoric　　　　　　　rhubarb

## K

The letter *k* is silent when it is the initial letter in a word, and is followed by *n*.

　　　know　　　　　　　knit

In certain instances a silent *k* helps to distinguish visually between homonyms. For example:

　　　night　　　　　　　not
　　　knight　　　　　　　knot

## L

The letter *l* is sometimes silent when it precedes another consonant within a syllable.

　　　calm　　　　　　　folk

## N

The letter *n* is silent when it follows *m* in a syllable.

　　　solemn　　　　　　　condemn

## P

The letter *p* is silent when it is the initial letter in a word, and is followed by *s*.

　　　psalm　　　　　　　psychology

## T

The letter *t* is silent when it precedes *ch* in a syllable.

　　　catch　　　　　　　pitch

The letter *t* is sometimes silent when it follows *s*.

listen                              castle

## W

When *w* follows *o* within a syllable, it is sometimes silent.

bowl                              low

### OTHER CONSONANTS

Other consonants, specifically *c, d, g, s,* and *x,* are more varied in the
sounds they record. Their most common sounds will be described here.
Comments about the sounds they record in combination with other letters will be found under the topic of Letter Combinations.

## C

The letter *c* has no phonetic value that is distinctly its own. Instead,
the two sounds it records are associated with other letters. One of these
sounds, called the "soft" sound of *c,* is usually associated with the letter
*s*. This soft sound can be heard in words like *cent* and *cymbal.* The other
sound recorded by *c,* and it is referred to as the "hard" sound, is generally associated with *k*. Illustrating this hard sound are words like
*cough* and *call.*

There are certain conditions under which each of the two sounds of
*c* predominates, and these are noted below:

When *c* is followed in a syllable by *e, i,* or *y,* it
usually has its soft sound.

certain                    city                    cylinder

When *c* is followed by any other letter, or is the
final letter in a syllable, it usually has its hard
sound.

cord                       fact                         arc

## X

The letter *x,* like the letter *c,* lacks a sound that is distinctly its own. However, it is used to record three different sounds, each of which is described below:

> A sound commonly recorded by *x* is best represented by the letter combination *ks.*

>       mix                axle

> Often, and especially when it is followed by a vowel or by a silent *h, x* records a sound represented by the letter combination *gz.*

>       exact           exhaust

> When *x* is the initial letter in a word—most of these will be highly technical words—it records the sound associated with the letter *z.*

>       xylophone      xylem

## G

Like *c,* the letter *g* also records sounds referred to as "soft" and "hard." The conditions under which each of these sounds predominates are as follows:

> When *g* is followed in a syllable by *e, i,* or *y,* it usually has its soft sound.

> gentle         ginger         gypsy

> When *g* is followed by any other letter, or is the final letter in a syllable, it usually has its hard sound.

> gallant         ghost         wig

Like the consonants referred to earlier, *g* can also be a silent letter. The most common instance of this is noted on the following page.

When *g* is followed in a syllable by *n*, it is silent.

gnat                              reign

## D

The letter *d* records two sounds. The first, and this is its usual sound, is heard in words like *do* and *wanted*. The other sound is like the sound associated with the letter *t,* and it is heard in such words as *picked* and *wrapped*. Those situations in which *d* assumes this second sound are best defined, and explained, by a reference to one of the classifications of sounds used by the phonetician.

In his technical analysis of sounds the phonetician refers to certain of the consonants as being voiced; to others as being unvoiced or voiceless. Such a classification is based on the state of the vocal cords when consonant sounds are made. More specifically, when *d, z, g, v,* and *b* are sounded, the vocal cords are drawn together and they vibrate. Consequently these consonants are referred to as the voiced consonants.

On the other hand, when *t, s, k, f,* and *p* are sounded, the vocal cords remain open and are "silent." These five consonants are thus referred to as voiceless consonants. According to a further classification, then, *t* is the voiceless counterpart of *d, s* the voiceless counterpart of *z, k* the voiceless counterpart of *g,* and so on. These counterparts are seen more clearly when the letters are shown as follows:

| *Voiced Consonants* | *Voiceless Counterparts* |
|:---:|:---:|
| d | t |
| z | s |
| g | k |
| v | f |
| b | p |

This classification of consonants can now be used to describe the instance in which the letter *d* assumes the sound associated with *t*.

When the consonant sound preceding *d* in a syllable is that of a voiceless consonant, the *d* sounds like a *t*.

missed                    kicked                    puffed

## S

Like the letter *d,* the letter *s* records two sounds. The first of these sounds is heard in words like *see, ask,* and *taps.* The other sound, heard in *heads* and *wags,* is like the sound of *z,* which is the voiced counterpart of *s.* The instance in which *s* sounds like the letter *z* is described below:

When the consonant sound preceding *s* in a syllable is not one of the voiceless consonants, the *s* assumes the sound associated with the letter *z.*

suds            tugs            cabs            pans

## LONG AND SHORT VOWELS

For the phonetician, the terms "long vowel" and "short vowel" refer to the duration of a vowel sound within a word. According to his classification, for example, the letter *e* has a long sound in *be,* but a short sound in *beet.* Or, to cite another example, the letter *o* would have a long sound in *road* and a shorter sound in *rote.*

In phonics, to the contrary, the terms "long vowel" and "short vowel" have come to refer to particular sounds. The long vowel sounds are those heard in the initial part of *age, eat, ice, open,* and *use.* The short vowel sounds are heard at the beginning of words like *ask, end, in, on,* and *up.* Because these ten sounds are the sounds most often recorded by the vowels, they are given special emphasis in phonics instruction.

With each vowel having two major sounds, it is important for the child to know the conditions under which each predominates. These conditions are described by generalizations in which the syllable is seen as the unit of pronunciation:

When there is one vowel in a syllable, and it does not come at the end of that syllable, it is usually short.

at            blend            candid            plastic

When there is one vowel in a syllable, and it
comes at the end of that syllable, it is usually
long.

go            she            solo            music

When there are two vowels within a syllable,
the first is usually long and the second silent.

cube        meat        hailstone        keepsake

Because this last generalization is very often concerned with words in
which the second of the two vowels is a final *e*, some teachers like to develop another generalization that focuses on these words in particular.
It might be stated as follows:

When there are two vowels within a syllable,
the second of which is a final *e,* the first vowel
is usually long and the final *e* is silent.

rake            hole            plate            nine

The listing of these generalizations about vowel sounds in no way suggests they will always "work" in the analysis of an unknown word. In
fact there are so many exceptions to them that generalizations have been
made about the exceptions. These generalizations are noted below:

When *i* is the only vowel within a syllable and
it is followed in the syllable by *ld, nd,* or *gh,* it
is usually long.

wild                        find                        sight

When *o* is the only vowel within a syllable and
it is followed in the syllable by *ld,* it is usually
long.

old                        behold                        scold

When a syllable ends in *nce* or *dge,* the preceding vowel is usually short.

fence        prince        badge        fudge

When a syllable ends in *ous,* the *ou* assumes the
short sound of *u.*

jealous                 dangerous                 callous

When the letter combination *ie* is found within
a syllable, the *i* is very often silent and the *e* is
long.

field            chief            piece            mien

When the letter combination *ei* appears within
a syllable and does not follow *c,* it often assumes the sound of long *a.*

freight                 vein                 weight

## THE LETTER Y FUNCTIONING AS A VOWEL

Strictly speaking, the letter *y* is a consonant and it records the sound
heard in the initial part of words like *yes* and *year.* In many instances,
however, *y* records sounds associated with the vowels. For this reason,
the request "Name the vowels" is often answered by "*a, e, i, o, u,* and
sometimes *y.*" Comments about *y* functioning as a vowel follow:

When *y* is the final sound in a one-syllable
word, it usually records the long *i* sound.

by                      rye                      cry

When *y* is the final sound in a multisyllabic
word, it usually approaches the long *e* sound.

merry            quietly            heavy

When *y* is in the middle of a syllable that has
no vowel, it usually records the short *i* sound.

myth            system            lymph

One comment needs to be made about the second generalization noted
above. In most of the teacher's manuals accompanying basal readers,
mention will be made of *y* having the sound of a short *i* when it appears

at the end of a multisyllabic word. The generalization cited in this booklet suggests it has the long sound of *e*, and for the following reason:
When words like *merry* or *quietly* are pronounced alone, their final
sound approaches the long sound of *e;* but when they are spoken with
other words as, for example, "The merry child skipped along the road,"
the final sound is de-emphasized and is like the sound of a short *i*. Since
unfamiliar words are analyzed one at a time, even though they are part
of a phrase or sentence, the generalization cited in this book seems more
valid and more helpful.

## THE SCHWA SOUND OF THE VOWELS

In an earlier chapter, attention was given to some changes that have
occurred in the development of our language over centuries of time. In
that chapter, however, no mention was made of the gradual change that
has occurred in vowel sounds when these vowels appear in unaccented
syllables.

Over time, the sounds of vowels in unaccented syllables have been de-
emphasized and, in many instances, they have shifted to what is called the
*schwa* (ə) sound. Probably the best way to describe the schwa sound is
to say it is very much like an unstressed short *u* sound, and it is heard in
such words as *a*bout, tak*e*n, im*i*tate, butt*o*n, and col*u*mn. Here, examples are easy to find because of the frequency of the schwa sound in our
language. Any page in a dictionary will quickly verify this.

Occurring with less frequency is the shift of vowel sounds, again in unaccented syllables, to the sound of a short *i* (d*e*bate, bagg*a*ge). Although
of less importance, because it occurs less frequently, this change too
should be noted in phonics instruction. Otherwise, when attention is not
given to de-emphasized vowel sounds, the pronunciation of words resulting from phonic analysis can be very artificial. In some instances,
the pronunciation might be sufficiently artificial that the child fails to
recognize the word as one in his listening or speaking vocabulary.

## LETTER COMBINATIONS

What precedes or follows a letter within a syllable often affects the
sound of that letter. Consequently, phonics instruction ought to give
attention to certain letter combinations that occur frequently in our language, and that have their own peculiar sounds.

In this book, discussion about letter combinations will proceed by giving attention to consonant combinations, consonant–vowel combinations and, finally, to vowel combinations.

## CONSONANT COMBINATIONS

The two kinds of consonant combinations stressed in phonics are called consonant digraphs and consonant blends. A digraph, according to the phonetician, is a combination of two letters that records a sound unlike that of either of the individual letters. To distinguish the digraph from the diphthong—the term "diphthong" will be discussed later—the phonetician also points out that when a digraph is sounded, the shape of the mouth does not change during the sounding process. For phonics, the important point is that a digraph is a two-letter combination recording a sound unlike that of either letter.

In our language the letter *h* is generally a part of consonant digraphs; it appears in the digraphs *ch, ph, sh, th,* and *gh.* The sounds of these five digraphs and, in some instances, the variability of their sounds, are illustrated below:

ch (chap, chef)
ph (phone, Stephen)
th (the, thin)
sh (she)
gh (rough)

One more consonant digraph, the letter combination *ng,* is commonly found at the end of a word. The sound it records is illustrated in *sing* and *rang.*

Other combinations of consonants appear in our language so frequently that, even though the sound of each consonant is maintained, they are usually emphasized together as the blending of two—in a couple of instances three sounds. They are thus referred to as consonant blends, and include:

| bl | fl | sc | st |
|----|----|----|-----|
| br | fr | sk | sw |
| cl | gl | sl | tr |
| cr | gr | sm | tw |
| dr | pl | sn | scr |
| dw | pr | sp | str |

## VOWEL–CONSONANT COMBINATIONS

Three consonants usually affect the sounds of the vowels when they follow these vowels within a syllable. They are *r, w,* and *l.*

The most frequent sounds of the vowels, when they are followed by *r,* are illustrated below:

> art, dollar
> her
> dirt
> nor, doctor
> fur

When *r* is preceded in a syllable by *a, e, i,* or, *u,* but is also followed by *e,* other sounds result. These sounds are illustrated in the following words:

> care
> mere
> fire
> sure

The consonant *w* sometimes follows *a* or *e* or *o* within a syllable. When it does, it also affects the sounds of these vowels. Illustrating the change are words like the following:

> law
> few
> now

The consonant *l* is more limited in its effect upon vowel sounds; it affects only the letter *a.* The "broad" sound it gives to an *a* is illustrated in words like *tall* and *always.*

## CONSONANT–VOWEL COMBINATIONS

The sounds of vowels are also affected by certain consonants that precede them within a syllable. Instances of this are described below:

> When the letter *u* is preceded within a syllable by *d* or *t,* the resulting sound of the *du* or *tu* is a kind of slurring sound best represented by the letters *joo* or *choo.*
>
> educate        gradual        mutual        punctuate

When *i* is preceded within a syllable by *c, s,* or
*t,* and it is followed by another vowel, the
resulting sound of the *ci* or *si* or *ti* is like the
sound commonly associated with the digraph *sh*.

facial                     mission                    action

One other consonant–vowel combination also merits attention:

In our language the letter *q* is always followed
by *u*. Together, the *q* and *u* record either the
sound associated with *kw,* or with the letter *k*
alone.

queen        acquire        bouquet        conquer

## VOWEL–VOWEL COMBINATIONS

Individual vowels are highly variable in the sounds they record. Combinations of these vowels are even more variable, and therefore more
difficult to cope with in the analysis of unfamiliar words. However, certain of the generalizations already cited do provide help, or at least a
starting point in correctly identifying the sounds of vowel combinations.
This is illustrated in the following generalizations:

When there are two vowels within a syllable,
the first is usually long and the second silent.

meat            coast            hail            keep

When a syllable ends in *ous,* the *ou* assumes the
short sound of *u*.

jealous            dangerous            callous

When the letter combination *ie* is found within
a syllable, the *i* is very often silent and the *e*
long.

chief                mien                diesel

When the letter combination *ei* appears within
a syllable and does not follow *c,* it often assumes the sound of long *a*.

freight            vein                weight

In thinking about the sounds of vowel–vowel combinations it might be helpful to see, as a whole, the combinations that are possible. Theoretically, the five vowels in our alphabet constitute twenty-five different vowel combinations. All of these combinations are listed below:

| | | | | |
|---|---|---|---|---|
| aa | ea | ia | oa | ua |
| ae | ee | ie | oe | ue |
| ai | ei | ii | oi | ui |
| ao | eo | io | oo | uo |
| au | eu | iu | ou | uu |

Because *y* so often functions as a vowel, it allows for five other vowel–vowel combinations:

| | | | | |
|---|---|---|---|---|
| ay | ey | iy | oy | uy |

Even a quick glance at these thirty possible combinations suggests that twelve are not the kinds of letter patterns generally found within syllables of American English words. Consequently, they need not be considered. The following eighteen vowel–vowel combinations then remain:

| | | | |
|---|---|---|---|
| ai | ea | oa | ue |
| au | ee | oe | ui |
| ay | ei | oi | uy |
|    | eu | oo |    |
|    | ey | ou |    |
|    | ie | oy |    |

Some of these eighteen combinations have only one pronunciation. Others commonly record two and even three sounds each. One combination, that of *o* and *u,* records as many as six sounds. All of this variability is more clearly seen in the listing on page 73. There, each word listed illustrates a sound recorded by a particular vowel–vowel combination. The starred words also illustrate, however, that certain of these sounds could be arrived at through the use of phonic generalizations already cited in this chapter. The remaining words in the list can only suggest once again that phonic generalizations are most helpful when seen as starting points in the analysis of a word, not as infallible guides to correct pronunciation.

## VOWEL–VOWEL COMBINATIONS

### I

ay  (say*)
ee  (meet*)
eu  (feud)
oa  (coat*)
oi  (oil)
oy  (toy)
uy  (buy)

### II

au  (auto, laugh)
ey  (they, honey*)
oe  (toe*, shoe)
ue  (cue*, sue)

### III

ai  (paid*, aisle, said)
ea  (each*, steak, dead)
ei  (either*, height, eight*)
ie  (pie*, chief*, friend)
oo  (book, pool, flood)
ui  (built, guise, suit)

### IV

ou  (out, ought, dough*,
     soup, cautious*, could)

## DIPHTHONGS

Four of the vowel–vowel combinations listed above are usually referred to as diphthongs. These are the combinations *oi, oy, ey,* and *ou* as heard in the words *oil, toy, they,* and *out*. Other diphthongs would be *ew* (few) and *ow* (cow); in these, *w* functions as a vowel.

According to the phonetician, a diphthong is a single sound recorded by two successive vowels within a syllable. But a diphthong is also defined as a kind of sound which, in the process of being made, requires a change in the mouth position.

For phonics, the most useful definition of diphthong is that it refers to the sound of a vowel–vowel combination which is unlike the sound of either of the individual vowels. A diphthong can then be thought of as the vowel counterpart of a digraph. For example:

| *Digraphs* | | *Diphthongs* | |
|---|---|---|---|
| ch | (chap) | oi | (oil) |
| ph | (phone) | oy | (toy) |
| th | (they) | ey | (they) |
| sh | (shoe) | ou | (out) |
| gh | (cough) | ow | (cow) |
| ng | (rang) | ew | (few) |

In phonics, attention to diphthongs is important not only because of their particular sounds but because they function as a single vowel when phonic generalizations are being applied. For example, if two unfamiliar words were *noise* and *choice,* the *oi* combination in each would function as a single vowel. As a result, the *oi* would have its diphthong sound, and the final *e* would be silent.

### SYLLABIFICATION

Phonic analysis of a word begins with the division of that word into syllables. Once the word is correctly divided, phonic generalizations can then be applied to each syllable. Following this, letter sounds within a syllable are blended and, in turn, the syllables themselves are joined to form the total word. The syllable thus functions as the unit of pronunciation. Because of this, some knowledge about syllabification is a prerequisite to advanced skill in phonics.

When unfamiliar words are spoken, their syllables can be identified orally. In the written version of unfamiliar words, however, syllables have to be identified visually; that is, through the use of visual cues. In this case the visual cues are particular letter arrangements. Consequently, like most of the generalizations in phonics, those concerned with syllabification also focus on the arrangement of letters within a word.

The most helpful generalizations about syllabification are given here.

> When two consonants appear between two
> vowels, a syllable division is usually made be-
> tween the consonants.

> num ber            ac cent            scar let

In using this generalization, it is important to keep in mind that consonant digraphs—for example, *sh* and *ch*—and also consonant blends
usually remain within the same syllable. This kind of "exception" might
be stated as follows:

> When two consonants appear between two
> vowels, and these consonants are either digraphs
> or blends, they very often remain within the
> same syllable.

> a shamed            ma chine            se cret

Another generalization that can be helpful in dividing words into syllables is the following:

> When a single consonant is preceded and fol-
> lowed by vowels, that consonant is usually in
> the same syllable as the vowel following it.

> e lect            be gan            u nite

A special generalization has to be made for the letter *x* when it is preceded and followed by a vowel. This could be stated as follows:

> When the letter *x* is preceded and followed by
> vowels, it is usually in the same syllable as the
> preceding vowel.

> tax i            ox en            ex am

> When a word ends in *le,* and the *le* is preceded
> by a consonant, that consonant usually forms a
> syllable with the *le.*

> ta ble            crip ple            gar gle

Prefixes and suffixes generally form separate syllables.

un wise                 shoe less                 re do ing

Special generalizations would have to be made for the suffix *ed:*

When the suffix *ed* is preceded by *d* or *t*, it forms a separate syllable.

want ed                 band ed                 com fort ed

When *ed* is not preceded by *d* or *t*, it does not form a separate syllable.

worked                  crowned                 banged

## ACCENT

Spoken language, if listened to attentively, shows periodic stresses. For example, the phrase *in the first place* would often be spoken with special stress given to the word *first*.

Similar kinds of stress patterns, or accents, are also found within single words. The word *independent*, for instance, follows the same stress pattern as the phrase *in the first place*. This is shown below:

in the first' place

in de pen' dent

Locating the syllables in a word that get this special stress is part of the job involved in arriving at the correct pronunciation of the word. Consequently some discussion about accented syllables is pertinent in any complete discussion of phonics and word analysis.

Unfortunately the stress patterns of American English words show as much variation as do the sounds of their letters. There are even some words, such as *detail* and *address,* for which a pattern has not yet been definitely established. Here again different kinds of factors account for the variability. For example, when a word and its derived forms have come into our language via Anglo-Saxon, the stress or accent tends to be on the root of the word. This would be illustrated in *love, lovely, lovable,* and *loveliness.* In words of Greek or Latin origin, to the contrary, the stress tends to shift as the word lengthens. This could be seen in words like *equal, equality, equalization,* and *equalitarian.*

That grammatical function affects the pronunciation of certain words is still another factor accounting for variability in accented syllables. The following sentences would show this:

> He was thought to be a *rebel,* but
> when the time came he did not *rebel.*

> The *content* of the book was so interest-
> ing that it left her feeling *content.*

In spite of these kinds of irregularities, generalizations regarding the location of accented syllables are available. One of the most frequently cited generalizations, for example, suggests that the first syllable in two-syllable words is the accented syllable; and this works well in many cases. But if the second of these syllables is also the root of the word (return, dethrone), another generalization takes precedence. This is one suggesting that in derived or inflected forms of words, the accent usually falls on or within the root.

While such complexities as these do exist, the position taken in this book is that some knowledge of generalizations about accents *can* be helpful to the child in his reading, and that a knowledge of them *is* helpful when they are used as starting points, not as infallible rules. For this reason, generalizations about locating accented syllables are given below:

> In most two-syllable words, the first syllable is
> usually accented.

| music | column | pencil |

> In derived or inflected forms of words, the ac-
> cent usually falls on or within the root of the
> word.

| recall | undoing | abnormal |

When the first vowel in a word is followed by
a double consonant, the first syllable is usually
the accented syllable.

happiness                article              sacrifice

Sometimes this generalization is superseded by one that suggests:

Syllables containing long vowel sounds are
often accented.

appliance              complete              stampede

Fortunately the final comment to be made about locating accented
syllables is more positive than earlier comments. It is the reminder that
a knowledge of the sounds of syllables in a word is often sufficient to
suggest which of these syllables is the accented one. To be more specific,
let us suppose that a child is acquainted with the word *pendulum* in its
spoken version. Let us suppose, too, that the first time he sees *pendulum*
in its written form he attempts to read it with the help of phonic analysis. If this analysis gives him the sounds of the three syllables, these
sounds will then be enough to suggest what the word is and, consequently, which of its syllables is to be accented. In such a case, obviously, the use of generalizations about accented syllables is unnecessary,
and would only get in the way and even slow down the child's attempt
to "figure out the word" on his own.

# 6

## *Some Final Comments about Phonics*

To know anything with thoroughness is to know it in all of its complexities. And sometimes the complexities seem overwhelming. This brief postscript, therefore, is directed to the teacher who now feels somewhat overwhelmed by "Phonics and the Teaching of Reading." To offer him a word of encouragement and comfort is its only purpose.

One very important and also comforting point to be made is that skill in phonics is not expected to be taught overnight. Instead, it is a skill that begins in kindergarten or first grade, but grows and matures throughout all of the grades. As one student teacher put it so well, "I imagine it's like raising a family. You take the problems one at a time, and then it's never quite so bad as when you think about all of them at once." So it is with phonics. Problems do come up, but usually one at a time. When taken one at a time they can be resolved, and out of the resolution comes a greater understanding of our language and of the way it is recorded.

Another point to keep in mind is that not all of the content of phonics is necessarily for all children. There might be some children who would find it easier to remember, for example, that *v, e, i, n* record the word *vein* than to remember the generalization which suggests that if the letter combination *ei* appears within a syllable, and does not follow *c,* often assumes the sound of long *a.*

On the other hand, there might also be children who could easily master all of the generalizations cited in this book, and then want to go on a "hunt" for still others. This too should be their prerogative.

And this leads to one final point. It might best be introduced with the comment of a second-grade teacher who was quick to admit she knew nothing beyond second-grade phonics and, here, "second-grade phonics" was what appeared in the teacher's manual accompanying a second-grade basal reader. One hope for this book is that it will give to teachers at all grade levels more complete knowledge of our language and of phonics. In this knowledge they should find security and also a basis for making decisions about the content of phonics they themselves will teach, and to which children they will teach it.

# 7

## Linguistics and Reading

"What is a linguistic approach to the teaching of reading?" This question is now asked with great frequency. Not too many years ago, a common sense kind of answer would probably have suggested that, since reading is one phase or dimension of language, any approach to the teaching of reading is necessarily "linguistic." Today, however, the answer must be more specific, because now a "linguistic approach" refers to proposals for reading instruction that come from linguists. Because some of these proposals concentrate on letter–sound relationships, a chapter on linguistics becomes pertinent in a book about phonics and the teaching of reading.

### WHAT IS LINGUISTICS?

One immediate difficulty in describing the field of linguistics is the variety of ways in which different linguists use identical terminology. This variation is found among Americans, and the variation only increases when comparisons are made between American and European linguists. Most linguists, however, would classify the concerns of their field of study under the headings of (1) Descriptive or Structural Linguistics, (2) Historical Linguistics, (3) Linguistic Geography, and (4) Comparative Linguistics.

*Descriptive linguistics*, the most basic branch of linguistic science, deals with the expression systems of language. Conventionally, descriptive linguistics is subdivided into phonology and grammar [6]. *Phonology* deals with the sound systems of languages, and also with the techniques for identifying and describing these sound features. While the primary focus is oral language, and this includes its intonation,

81

linguists concerned with phonology would be at least indirectly interested in the ways in which languages are recorded.

*Grammar*, the second subdivision of descriptive linguistics, is further divided into morphology and syntax. A brief description of *morphology* is to say it is a study of the minimal units of meaning in a language. In many instances these meaningful units, or "morphemes," are root words. In other instances, in American English, morphemes are prefixes and suffixes. Thus, *go* is a morpheme, and *-ing* is a morpheme, but *going* comprises two morphemes. A description of how these morphemes are put together in any given language goes under the heading of *syntax*, the second subdivision of grammar.

*Historical linguistics*, as the name suggests, concentrates on the changes in a language over time. *Linguistic geography*, on the other hand, is concerned with speech variations or dialects within a language at any given time. *Comparative linguistics*, the fourth major subdivision of linguistics mentioned earlier, is a study of the relationships among languages of common origin.

A listing of all of these various categories and subcategories of linguistics is given below:

**Linguistics**

1. *Descriptive Linguistics*
   Phonology
   Grammar
      Morphology
      Syntax
                        2. *Historical Linguistics*
                                    3. *Linguistic Geography*
                                                4. *Comparative Linguistics*

## DEVELOPMENT OF LINGUISTICS

Linguistics, as a scientific study of language, is hardly a new field. It has been active since at least the early part of the nineteenth century [5]; and if there is a willingness to define linguistics more broadly than is now done, it can even be said that there were linguists prior to the nineteenth century.

What *is* new, however, is the great interest in linguistics that is so apparent today. This interest is reflected in the number of students entering the field of linguistics. It is also reflected in the many anthropologists, sociologists, and psychologists who show a growing concern for language as a most important form of human behavior. Professional educators also show increased interest in linguistics—some because they are concerned about the teaching of grammar, others because they teach English as a second language, and still others because they are especially involved in the teaching of reading.

## LINGUISTICS AND THE TEACHING OF READING

In modern times, linguistics and reading were probably first brought together by Leonard Bloomfield in two articles that appeared in *Elementary English Review* in 1942 [2]. Since then, interest in linguistics as a possible source of help with the teaching of reading has increased greatly—first very slowly, then recently very quickly. Why the great interest?

Certainly one factor has been the increased activity of more and more linguists. This has led to a rapid expansion of literature in their field. In turn, linguistic theory and knowledge have become more accessible not only to linguists themselves but also to those outside the field.

Another factor accounting for the interest of educators in linguistics is the current emphasis on instruction in phonics as one important part of instruction in reading. Such emphasis naturally encourages interest in a field like linguistics, in which there has always been serious study of the sound features of language. It could also be said that the current concern for linguistics is one specific dimension of the larger and broader interest of educators in the various "disciplines." For all of these different reasons, then, linguistics as a possible source of help with reading has become a very popular topic.

## LINGUISTIC PROPOSALS FOR READING

While it is true that some individuals talk and write as if there were *a* linguistic approach to the teaching of reading, the specific pedagogical proposals being made by linguists hardly suggest such unity [3]. For example, in the Bloomfield articles referred to earlier [2], the proposal is to teach beginning reading by concentrating exclusively on carefully selected monosyllable words—both real and nonsense words—which show a particular spelling pattern.* By analogy, children are to deduce the sounds associated with particular letters.

Another linguist, Carl Lefevre, moves in a direction quite different from that of Bloomfield. Lefevre maintains that "individual words do not have the importance commonly attributed to them in reading instruction." He suggests that teachers should attend to larger groupings of words and that, from these larger units, "children would be expected to develop their own generalizations of spelling–sound relationships . . ." [9].

Still another linguist, Donald Lloyd, suggests that "the ability to relate the melody of speech to the written page is the key to good reading." Although this emphasis on intonation appears consistently in Lloyd's writings [10, 11], his specific proposals for teaching reading are still to come.

Other kinds of proposals have been made by other linguists—for example, reading texts should be devoid of pictures, the language of texts should be like the spoken language of children [7, 12]. However, there is no need to enumerate or describe all of them. The point to be emphasized here is that there is not one "linguistic approach to the teaching of reading," but many.

The linguistic approach most relevant in a book about phonics is best represented by the proposal of Bloomfield [2], referred to earlier, and the more recent proposal of Charles Fries [5]. The two proposals are not identical in detail but, in their emphasis on letter–sound (grapheme–phoneme) relationships, they are sufficiently similar to be classified as one kind of proposal. To describe either, however, a more detailed description of phonology must first be given.

## PHONOLOGY

As has already been mentioned, phonology is that branch of linguistics which concentrates on a scientific study of the speech sounds in human language. When the speech sounds of a given language are initially studied, these sounds are recorded carefully and in minute detail as they

---

* Bloomfield's phonological proposal, and others like his, are especially relevant in a book about phonics. They are examined in detail, beginning on page 86.

are articulated in speech. Such an analysis comes under the heading of "phonetics."

The next step in the phonological analysis of a language—and this comes under the heading of "phonemics"—is to group these phonetically recorded speech sounds into the "phonemes" of that language. This grouping or identification of phonemes is achieved through the "method of contrast" [5, 6].

*Phonemes*, according to the linguist, are classes of sounds identified by contrast. Phonemes are not separate sounds, and they cannot be pronounced in isolation. Rather, says the linguist, they are bundles of sound contrasts that find their realization in spoken words [5].

How phonemes are identified through contrast can be illustrated by a few combinations of words which linguists call "minimal pairs." For example:

|      |      |
|------|------|
| fill | pill |
| tab  | tap  |
| tot  | pot  |

In the first pair, the spoken forms of *fill* and *pill* differ in a minimal way; that is, by a single phoneme. In the contrast of *fill* and *pill*, therefore, two phonemes can be identified. To distinguish between phonemes (spoken language) and graphemes (written language), linguists enclose phoneme symbols in / /. Thus—to return to the examples—by contrasting the pronunciation of *fill* and *pill*, the phonemes /f/ and /p/ are identified. In contrasting the spoken forms of *tab* and *tap*, the phoneme /b/ is identified, and the phoneme /p/ is re-identified.

In the column of words listed above, the minimal pair *tot* and *pot* is useful in emphasizing that phonemes are associated with the sounds of language rather than with the ways these sounds are conventionally spelled. For, phonemically, *tot* and *pot* would be recorded, at least in some symbol systems, as /tat/ and /pat/ [6].*

With this very brief explanation, the following definition should now make sense: "The phoneme is the minimum feature of the expression system of a spoken language by which one thing that may be said is distinguished from any other thing which might have been said" [6].

---

* The vowel symbols used by linguists do not always correspond to the vowels appearing in a word.

No description of the phoneme would be complete without at least a brief reference to the term "allophone." According to the linguist, allophones are subclasses of sounds within a phoneme. For instance, the phoneme /k/ in *key* and in *ski* constitutes two different allophones. These allophones, evidently, are easily identified by linguists who have had much studied practice in hearing and analyzing subtle differences among sounds. For the untrained person, however, some of these sound-differences would be difficult if not impossible to hear. All of this is to say that Professor Higgins, the famous linguist in Shaw's *Pygmalion*, was not a person of just ordinary talent.

### THE PROPOSALS OF TWO LINGUISTS

In the 1940's, Leonard Bloomfield, a well-known linguist, made certain proposals for teaching beginning reading which, at least at first glance, bear some resemblance to the teaching of phonics [2]. Twenty years later his proposals were repeated in *Let's Read* [1], a book published posthumously in 1961 and edited by Clarence Barnhart, a lexicographer.

In another book, *Linguistics and Reading* [5], Charles Fries has suggested ways to teach beginning reading which are closely similar to the proposals of Bloomfield. However, the theory underlying the pro-posals of Fries is described in much greater detail than is the theory of Bloomfield. Consequently, the Fries text will be used here as the primary basis for describing and comparing the proposals of both linguists.

For both linguists, reading is a matter of learning to make high-speed recognition responses to the spelling patterns of a given language. But beginning reading, it is suggested by these two linguists, starts with the instant, automatic recognition of the letters of the alphabet. Fries maintains that the capital letters have simpler forms, and so they should be used first. Bloomfield, on the other hand, maintains that the capital and lower case letters should both be taught before reading is begun. Although there is this difference, both linguists agree that the method of contrast is the way to teach the alphabet. For example, Fries writes:

> For starting the reading process the beginner does not need to have a recognition control of the entire alphabet. Some of the letters occur much less frequently than others, as, for example, Q, Z, X, V, J. But the patterns

of those that occur in the first materials to be read must be *recognized in contrast with one another* without hesitation. In fact, the child is not ready for the "reading process" itself until he automatically responds to the contrastive graphic patterns that identify a sufficient body of the letters to be used. . . . [5; pp. 125-126]

Once the letters are recognized, Fries and Bloomfield both suggest that the next step in teaching reading is one that concentrates on high-speed recognition responses to the patterns of American English spelling. These patterns are introduced by carefully selected monosyllable words. Each word is identified, then contrasted with phonetically related words, also of one syllable.

The first spelling pattern introduced by Fries is a consonant–vowel–consonant pattern to emphasize consonant phonemes. Fries explains:

At the beginning and for considerable time thereafter the teacher pronounces in *normal talking fashion* each new word and each pair of contrastive words as it is introduced and makes sure that the pupil, from that pronunciation, identifies the words as ones he knows.

Only complete words are pronounced. The pronunciation for the "word" is thus attached to the total spelling-pattern that represents that word. The spelling-pattern *cat* represents the word /kæt/ as pronounced. Sounds are not given to the separate letters of a spelling-pattern. The understanding of the difference that any particular letter makes in the spelling-pattern is built up out of the experience of pronouncing a variety of word pairs with minimum differences in their *spelling-patterns*.

CAT — AT
CAT — RAT
CAT — PAT

We avoid completely such a question as "What does the letter *C* say?" [5; pp. 203-204]

The first spelling pattern, as Fries describes it, would include such words as *met*, *ship*, *rush*, *bang*, *mask*, *bran*, *pick*, *cuff*, and *call*. Once identified, these words would then be contrasted with other words like *pet*, *chip*, *lush*, *hang*, *task*, *clan*, *sick*, *muff*, and *wall*. Here the contrast is to teach the identification of consonant phonemes.

The second spelling pattern introduced by Fries is one in which a final *e* is used to differentiate it from the first pattern. For reading, the concentration in this second pattern is on vowel phonemes. Some examples of the second pattern, listed in contrast to examples from the first pattern, are as follows:

BAD    —  BADE
GRIP   —  GRIPE
BACK   —  BAKE
TALL   —  TALE

Three other groups of spelling patterns introduced by Fries have a more limited application, but also emphasize vowel phonemes. These groups are shown in the following listing, again in contrast with words from the first pattern:

MET    —  MEAT
BEST   —  BEAST
LAD    —  LAID
BALL   —  BAIL
ROD    —  ROAD
SOCK   —  SOAK

It is Fries's contention that these various patterns form the basis of American English spelling. He says also: "There are, of course, some other minor patterns than those noted here but for the beginning stages of reading it is the major sets of contrastive spelling-patterns that require the kind of practice that leads to high-speed recognition responses" [5; pp. 181-182].

What about the proposals of Bloomfield? Bloomfield, too, emphasizes spelling patterns and the method of contrast in teaching beginning reading [1]. However, Bloomfield's patterns are different from those suggested by Fries. They are also less precisely defined, and they cover a greater variety of words.

In the Bloomfield material, found in *Let's Read*, the first pattern emphasizes words comprised of a vowel and a consonant, or of a consonant plus a vowel plus another consonant. Within this pattern words like *tan*, *bag*, and *had* are taught. Next, words like *tin*, *big*, and *hid* are identified, then contrasted with the earlier words, *tan*, *bag*, *had*. This identification, followed by contrast, is to teach vowel phonemes. The process goes on for the first thirty-six lessons.

In the next series of lessons outlined in *Let's Read*, a second spelling pattern is introduced which deals with the "regular" sound values of nineteen consonants. In this series, speech forms (words) written with digraphs are included.

The third series of lessons in the Bloomfield text concentrates on words which have pairs of vowel letters, such as *ee* and *ea*, and on words which combine a vowel with either *y* or *w*.

The fourth series of lessons goes under the heading of "The Commonest Irregular Words." Here, words like *was*, *said*, and *been* are included. In the description of this series of lessons it is noted that:

> There is a great difference between the work of Lessons 1–97 (first three series of lessons) and almost all the child's later work in reading. Lessons 1–97 have taught him a system in which each letter or each combination of two letters represents always the same sound or sounds of his language.
>
> If our system of writing were completely phonetic, the rest of our work would consist simply of further practice in these habits. But our system of writing is not completely phonetic; the child has now the difficult task of forming a great many new and special habits for single words or classes of words in which the letters represent sounds other than those which he has so far learned. . . .
>
> In our work hitherto we have been dealing with common values of the letters; any word or even any nonsense syllable (such as *nim*, *nib*, etc.) which contains only letters in these normal values, is suitable for practice. When it comes to teaching irregular and special words, each word will demand a separate effort and separate practice. [1; p. 206]

The fifth series of lessons in the Bloomfield book is called "The Commonest Irregular Spellings of Vowel Sounds." In this series, words such as *safe*, *care*, *book*, and *room* are listed. The text's discussion of the word *safe* explains that:

> We call this an irregular spelling because we have taught the child when he sees a word with the letter *a* to produce the vowel sound of *hat, bat, mat*. We must now modify this habit and teach him, when he sees certain spellings with the letter *a*, to produce a different sound. [1; p. 284]

The sixth and final series of lessons in *Let's Read* is called "The Commonest Irregular Spellings of Consonant Sounds." Here, words like *cent*, *badge*, *knee*, *hour*, *phone*, and *calm* are introduced.

## LINGUISTIC PROPOSALS CONTRASTED WITH PHONICS

To clarify still further the proposals for teaching reading that have been made by Fries and Bloomfield, a comparison between their proposals and the method of teaching phonics described in this book will be made. Actually, some differences and similarities have already been indirectly noted. Now, however, a more systematic and explicit comparison should lead to a better understanding of the two proposals, and .of instruction in phonics too. This comparison will give attention to (1) some basic assumptions, (2) methods of study, and (3) selection of words to be taught.

### Some Basic Assumptions

That phonics and the two linguistic proposals both take advantage of the alphabetic nature of our written language is, of course, very obvious. Phonics emphasizes letter–sound relationships; the proposals of Fries and Bloomfield, letter–phoneme relationships. Side by side with this similarity, however, there is also a major difference. According to these linguists, phonemes cannot be sounded in isolation. Instead, as Fries explains repeatedly, phonemes find their realization in spoken words. As a result, the emphasis in the two linguistic proposals is on the pronunciation of words rather than on the sounds of parts of words.

What about phonics? As presented in this book, instruction in phonics assumes that a word is the close blending of smaller units of sound, and that these smaller units are associated with particular letters or letter-combinations. The assumption is also made that vowel sounds, when articulated outside the framework of a word and by a person not trained in phonology, appear to him to be closely identical to—as Fries puts it—their realization in a word. For this reason the recommendation was made in Chapter 3 of this book that the blending of sounds in a syllable which begins with a vowel can proceed in a left-to-right direction. For instance, if the written form of the word *ant* were not known to a child, he would be encouraged to blend its three sounds as:

$$\breve{a} \longrightarrow \breve{a}n \longrightarrow \breve{a}nt$$

In contrast with this assumption about vowel sounds, the phonic instruction proposed in this book clearly recognizes the "impurity" of sounds recorded by consonants, when these sounds are made apart from a syllable or word. (See page 49.) Consequently, it was recommended that the identification of a word like *man*—assuming no phonetically related word such as *an* or *fan* is known—would be achieved most easily by a blending of sounds that proceeds in the following sequence:

$$\text{ă} \longrightarrow \text{mă} \longrightarrow \text{măn}$$

## Methods of Study

An earlier discussion in this present chapter referred to the "method of contrast" as the way in which linguists carry on their study of the sound features of language. Consequently, it did not come as a surprise that the Fries–Bloomfield proposals for teaching beginning reading also emphasized contrast as the way to teach both the recognition of letters of the alphabet and, subsequently, the recognition of carefully selected words. In the Fries text, for example, it is noted that "the difference any particular letter makes . . . is built up out of the experience of pronouncing a variety of word pairs with minimum differences in their spelling–patterns" [5; p. 204]. Following this explanation there is a listing of:

CAT — AT
CAT — RAT
CAT — PAT

Later on in his text, and still emphasizing contrastive features as a way of identifying written words, Fries lists:

| | | |
|---|---|---|
| MAN | MANE | MEAN |
| DAN | DANE | DEAN |
| BAN | BANE | BEAN |
| HAT | HATE | HEAT |
| FAT | FATE | FEAT |
| MAT | MATE | MEAT |

In his discussion of these groupings of words Fries writes:

Instead of the approach through trying to match individual letters and separate sound units, we must develop the automatic habits of responding to the contrastive features of *spelling-patterns as identifying the word-patterns* they represent. For example, even in the three letter word used above, *man*, it is not the single letter *A* that indicates the vowel sound [æ]. It is the spelling-pattern *man* in contrast with the spelling-pattern *mane* or that of *mean* that signals the different vowel phonemes that make these three different words. [5; p. 200]

How do the teaching procedures of phonics differ from the linguist's method of contrast, as exemplified in this passage from Fries's book? Or, do they differ?

Inductive phonics, the kind recommended in this book, makes use of the words a child knows to identify for him the sounds which letters record. For example, a child's familiarity with the written form of words like the following could be used to identify the sound commonly recorded by *t*:

> to
> turn
> take
> ten

When a teacher uses words like *to*, *turn*, *take*, and *ten* to help a child identify the sound generally recorded by the letter *t*, could this be called a "method of contrast"? If such a method includes a comparison of similarities as well as of differences, then the procedures of inductive phonics that concentrate on visual–auditory similarities in words could be characterized as contrastive.

More obviously in the category of contrast, however, is the use of selected words, in phonics, to define the conditions under which the various sounds recorded by particular letters predominate. For instance, the following comparison of words is useful in showing the effect of the number of vowels in a syllable on the sounds recorded by these vowels:

> at        ate
> met       meet
> ran       rain
> pin       pine
> mad       made

To suggest, here, that a method of contrast is used in inductive phonics is not to suggest, too, that linguists such as Fries and Bloomfield would give hearty approval to the teaching procedures recommended in this book. Actually, both have been very explicit in their criticism of phonics.

For example, Fries has written:

> The assumption that learning to read is learning to match words, as written, letter by letter, with words, as pronounced, sound by sound, constitutes the basic difficulty with *phonics* as a method of teaching reading. . . . In spite of the widespread familiarity of the "phonics" way of approaching reading and its continuous use we must cast it out here for a more thoroughly successful way. [5; pp. 199-200]

## Selection of Words to Be Taught

According to Fries, and according to Bloomfield too, one reason for the success of their teaching procedures is the way they select a reading vocabulary. The following passage from Bloomfield's *Let's Read* discusses the selection of words:

> When the letters and the left-to-right order have been thoroughly mastered, we are ready to begin reading. In the words to be read during the first stage every letter must represent only and always one single phoneme. . . . This task (reading) is sufficiently difficult; we must not make it even more difficult by introducing irregular spellings before the basic habit is set up. . . . [1; p. 36]

On the basis of this and other passages in the Bloomfield and Fries texts, how would these two linguists react to a recommendation made earlier in this chapter; namely, that words like *to*, *turn*, *take*, and *ten* could be used to help children identify the sound associated with the letter *t*? Here, comments about the probable reactions of Bloomfield and Fries will be helpful in differentiating between the selection of words they recommend, and the selection that might be used in instruction in phonics. These comments will also serve to show that the two linguists themselves do not always agree on what constitutes "regular" and "irregular" spellings.

To begin, then, how would Bloomfield and Fries react to the early use of the word *to*? Actually, both linguists would probably be critical. Because of the sound recorded by the letter *o* in this word, Bloomfield would classify *to* as having an irregular spelling; this is in contrast to the "regular" spelling of a word like *tot*. Fries, too, would object to the early use of the word *to* because it does not fit into what he calls the major spelling patterns of English. It is important to note here, however, that within each of the patterns described by Fries the same letter is not always associated with the same sound—or, as he would say, the same phoneme. In Fries's first major pattern, for instance, words like *buff* and *bull* are both included. Yet the vowel *u* hardly records the same sound in the two words, even though in both there is a consonant–vowel–consonant pattern. It could certainly be asked: Why should a word like *bull* be taught early, but not the much more useful word *to*? In this instance the rationale underlying Fries's categories of patterns offers no explanation. It can surely be suggested, though, that the sound recorded by *u* in *bull* is just as "irregular" as the sound recorded by *o* in *to*.

But, to move on, what about the use of a word like *turn*? Words such as *turn*, in which the sound recorded by the vowel is affected by the letter *r*, are never mentioned in the Fries text. From such silence it could be assumed that *turn* would be classified as "irregular." The Bloomfield text is more explicit. In the fifth series of lessons in *Let's Read*, *turn* is specifically listed under the category of "The Commonest Irregular Spellings of Vowel Sounds."

Comments of both Bloomfield and Fries about the selection of a word like *take* for a beginning reading vocabulary are very predictable. Bloomfield considers as irregular the spelling of *take* because "we have taught the child when he sees a word with the letter *a* to produce the vowel sound of *hat, bat, mat*" [1; p. 284]. Fries, to the contrary, would classify the spelling of *take* as representing one of the major patterns in American English.

Reactions to the use of the word *ten* are predictable and, in this instance, identical. Bloomfield would classify the spelling of *ten* as regular, and Fries would classify its spelling as an example of a major pattern used in our language. Consequently, both linguists would approve of the early introduction of the word *ten* in developing a child's reading vocabulary.

## A CRITIQUE OF THE LINGUISTIC PROPOSALS

This concluding note of probable approval on the part of Bloomfield and Fries should not de-emphasize the many criticisms of phonics made by both of these linguists. Nor should the note of approval de-emphasize the need to look, and with a critical eye, at the proposals of Bloomfield and Fries. With controlled and objective evaluation still lacking, the following reactions to their proposals are primarily for the purpose of raising questions.

## Monosyllable Words

In many instances the most spontaneous questions are those that ask for more information about the proposals. For example, the Fries text deals only with monosyllable words and, in fact, just those monosyllable words that fit into certain spelling patterns. This very narrow concern immediately raises questions about the teaching of multisyllable words.

At one point in his discussion, Fries notes:

> The word-patterns represented by this very large set of spelling patterns are all single syllable words. But these syllables occur very frequently as parts of multisyllable words. [5; p. 177]

In a discussion about the use of nonsense syllables, a similar note of optimism, and oversimplification, appears in the Bloomfield book:

> If the child is worried by the fact that these nonsense syllables are meaningless, you may point out to him that they are part of longer words which he will learn later; that is, *han* is the first part of the word *handle*, *jan* is part of *January*, *mag* is part of *magnet* and *magpie*. [1; p. 59]

The obvious problem, of course, is that the combination of letters in the syllable *mag* is also found in words like *magic* and *magistrate*. Yet, the sound of *mag* is not retained in these two words, because *m* and *a* are in one syllable while the letter *g* is in another. Neither the Fries nor the Bloomfield proposals deal specifically with syllables, though in phonics the syllable is considered the basic unit of pronunciation.

## Amount of Practice Required

One reason for Fries's concentration on monosyllable words of a given kind is that he sees beginning reading as high-speed responses to the patterns of American English spelling. Fries recognizes the great amount of practice required for developing these responses, but Bloomfield mentions it with greater frequency. At one point, for example,

Bloomfield writes, "The early reading lessons should not be very long, for they demand a severe intellectual effort" [1; p. 41]. A few paragraphs later, in a discussion about teaching words like *can* and *fan*, Bloomfield offers this reminder: "All we do is to present such words together; the resemblance of sound and spelling will do its work without any explanation from us. Only, we must remember that this takes a great deal of time and repetition" [1; p. 42].

Those who have had classroom teaching experience, and especially those who have worked with young children, might certainly question both the desirability and the possibility of using a method of teaching beginning reading which requires such large amounts of practice—even practice to the extent that words must be "overlearned" [1; p. 58]. To be admired is the honesty with which these linguists admit that success with their proposals demands much practice and repetition. However, admiration does not prevent one from asking, and with haste, "Is all of this possible when a classroom teacher is working with young children?" For the teacher, what is possible and practical is just as important as what is theoretically correct.

## Tight Control of Reading Vocabulary

In addition to the requirement of large amounts of practice, the proposals of both Fries and Bloomfield also depend upon a tightly controlled reading vocabulary. Such a stipulation raises a question about the compatibility of their proposals with the fact that young children, long before they ever enter school, are exposed to many written words that hardly adhere to either Bloomfield's or Fries's rigid prescriptions [4]. And what about Fries's insistence that the reading of numerals be postponed because they distract from the alphabetic nature of our writing system [5; p. 128]? Does this take into account the many preschool children who quickly learn to identify the numbers found on TV dials, calendars, clocks, elevators, receipts, and street signs? Certainly nobody —linguist or otherwise—would ever want to discourage the great interest that many young children have in the letters, the numbers, and the words that constantly surround them in their everyday world. Yet Fries and Bloomfield make no allowance for this kind of curiosity as they lay down more and more stipulations about the words to be taught in beginning reading.

## Dependence upon Analogy

In teaching their highly prescribed vocabulary, both Fries and Bloomfield depend upon analogy as the way in which children will come to associate particular words with particular combinations of letters. For instance, Bloomfield writes:

> When we present a pair of words like *can* and *fan*, a child may have no notion that these words are similar in sound, or that the similar spelling indicates a similar sound. It would be a waste of time to try, as do the advocates of "phonic" methods, to explain this to him. All we do is present such words together; the resemblance of sound and spelling will do its work without any explanation from us. [1; p. 42]

A passage in the Fries text, one cited earlier in this chapter, also gives emphasis to analogy rather than to explanation as a way of teaching letter–sound relationships:

> The understanding of the difference that any particular letter makes in the spelling-pattern is built up out of the experience of pronouncing a variety of word pairs with minimum differences in their *spelling-patterns:* CAT–AT; CAT–RAT; CAT–PAT. [5; p. 204]

These pronouncements of Bloomfield and Fries tempt everyone with elementary school teaching experience to wonder about the ability of all children to grasp letter–sound relationships merely by analogy. These pronouncements and, in addition, the words selected to serve as examples of the vocabulary to be taught, also tempt a teacher to question the usefulness of the method of analogy in teaching words that fail to fit into prescribed spelling patterns. Fries never really deals with "misfits." When Bloomfield does, the method of analogy seems to disappear into the background, although the unimportant role assigned to "explanation" remains. For example, in discussing a series of lessons, in *Let's Read*, Bloomfield writes:

> In most of the words . . . the letter *a* is followed by a single consonant letter, and this, in turn, by a silent *e*, as in *cake, cape, game, safe.* . . . Some other words of the present section have the letter *a* followed by a single consonant letter which in turn is followed by *le*, as in *table, cradle.* Others have *a* followed by a single consonant letter with suffixal *y* after it, as *lady, gravy.* In short, we could state some rules about English spelling which

would cover these words. . . . To be sure, these rules would be rather complicated. We shall not try to explain such things to the child. [1; p. 284]

Passages like this one from the Bloomfield text raise still more questions about the ability of all children to learn to read by a so-called "linguistic method." In addition, a passage like this, especially when considered in conjunction with various others in the text, makes it difficult to see the difference between Bloomfield's approach to "irregular" words, and the "whole word method" which both he and Fries are so quick to criticize.

### POSSIBLE CONTRIBUTIONS OF LINGUISTS

The notes of pessimism in this critique of the Bloomfield–Fries proposals are not designed to lessen the hope that linguists will help to improve the teaching of reading. Whether suggestions for better teaching come from the linguist or, for example, from the psychologist, they should be welcomed—but their value for instruction must be proved, not just assumed. The gap that exists between what is correct in theory and what "works" in the classroom can be wide, and so the steps across the gap should be evaluated all along the way. Until the steps suggested by both Bloomfield and Fries are tried out in a variety of classrooms, and until the results are then carefully evaluated, not much more can be done than to continue to raise questions about the proposals.

Meanwhile, though, there are important and needed contributions to teacher education that would be natural for linguists to make. For instance, it is the linguist who can help classroom teachers gain competence in developing newer kinds of language study. Even at the elementary school level, attention could be given to the history of our language, to the factors that have affected its development, to the histories of individual words, and to the ways in which pronunciation and meanings of words have changed over time. For too long the most interesting aspects of language study have been unknown to teachers, and therefore unavailable to children. Yet, with books and with college courses, linguists could bring this study into focus. Some good books have already been written; a few, for both teachers and children, are listed at the end of Chapter I in this book. However, there is the need and certainly the room for many more.

Another area to which linguists can contribute is that of teaching bilingual children to read. Here the need is not so much for a particular method of teaching as it is for accurate information about the major similarities and differences in the writing systems and in the grammatical structures of the child's two languages. How very helpful it would be, for instance, if simply written but highly accurate books were available which outlined language contrasts. With this information, at least some of the special problems of bilingual children could be predicted and, as a result, avoided.

But linguists can also help with reading in the case of children whose native tongue is English. In this instance the linguist could offer much more guidance than he has thus far given in helping teachers organize and systematize, for themselves and ultimately for the children they teach, both the regularities and the irregularities found in the writing system of our language. Fries begins to offer help of this kind when he discusses the linguist's interest in "grapheme" (letter) sequences in the various languages. Fries notes:

> In English, for example, the last consonant of the word *king* never occurs initially in a word.* It always comes after a vowel. In English, there are at least 100 different consonant clusters that occur at the ends of words, as /nd/ in *sand* . . . ; /lt/ in *wilt*. . . . And there are at least 40 other consonant clusters that occur at the beginnings of words, as /gl/ in *glad* . . . ; /br/ in *bread*. . . . But of all of these clusters, only three—/st/, /sp/, /sk/—occur both at the beginnings and at the ends of words. . . . [5; p. 67]

With even more systematic information of this kind, reading instruction—and especially instruction in phonics—could become so much more productive, if only because it would be so much more organized, complete, and knowledgeable. We look to linguists for more help of this kind.

### REFERENCES

1. Bloomfield, L., and Barnhart, C. L. *Let's Read*. Detroit: Wayne State University Press, 1961.
2. Bloomfield, Leonard. "Linguistics and Reading." *Elementary English Review*, XIX (April–May 1942), 125-130, 183-186.

* The "consonant" to which Fries refers is the consonant digraph *ng*.

3. Durkin, Dolores. "Linguistics and the Teaching of Reading." *The Reading Teacher,* XVI (March 1963), 342-346.

4. ————. "Children Who Read before Grade 1: A Second Study." *Elementary School Journal,* LXIV (December 1963), 143-148.

5. Fries, Charles C. *Linguistics and Reading.* New York: Holt, Rinehart and Winston, Inc., 1963.

6. Gleason, H. A. *Descriptive Linguistics* (Revised Edition). New York: Holt, Rinehart and Winston, 1961.

7. Hall, Robert A. *Sound and Spelling in English.* Philadelphia: Chilton Company, 1961.

8. Lefevre, Carl A. *Linguistics and the Teaching of Reading.* New York: McGraw-Hill Book Company, 1964.

9. ————. "Reading Instruction Related to Primary Language Learnings: A Linguistic View." *Journal of Developmental Reading* (Spring 1961), 147-158.

10. Lloyd, Donald. "Intonation and Reading." *Education,* LXXXIV (May 1964), 538-541.

11. ————. *Reading American English Sound Patterns.* A Monograph for Elementary Teachers—No. 104. Evanston, Illinois: Row, Peterson, 1962.

12. Strickland, Ruth G. *The Language of Elementary School Children: Its Relationship to the Language of Reading Textbooks and the Quality of Reading of Selected Children.* Bloomington: Indiana University, 1962.